Drawing Nature

THIS BOOK
BELONGS TO

....

....

....

Drawing Nature

WRITTEN AND
ILLUSTRATED BY
VIKTORIJA
SEMJONOVA

100 Prompts, Projects & Playful Exercises

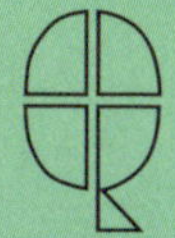

quadrille

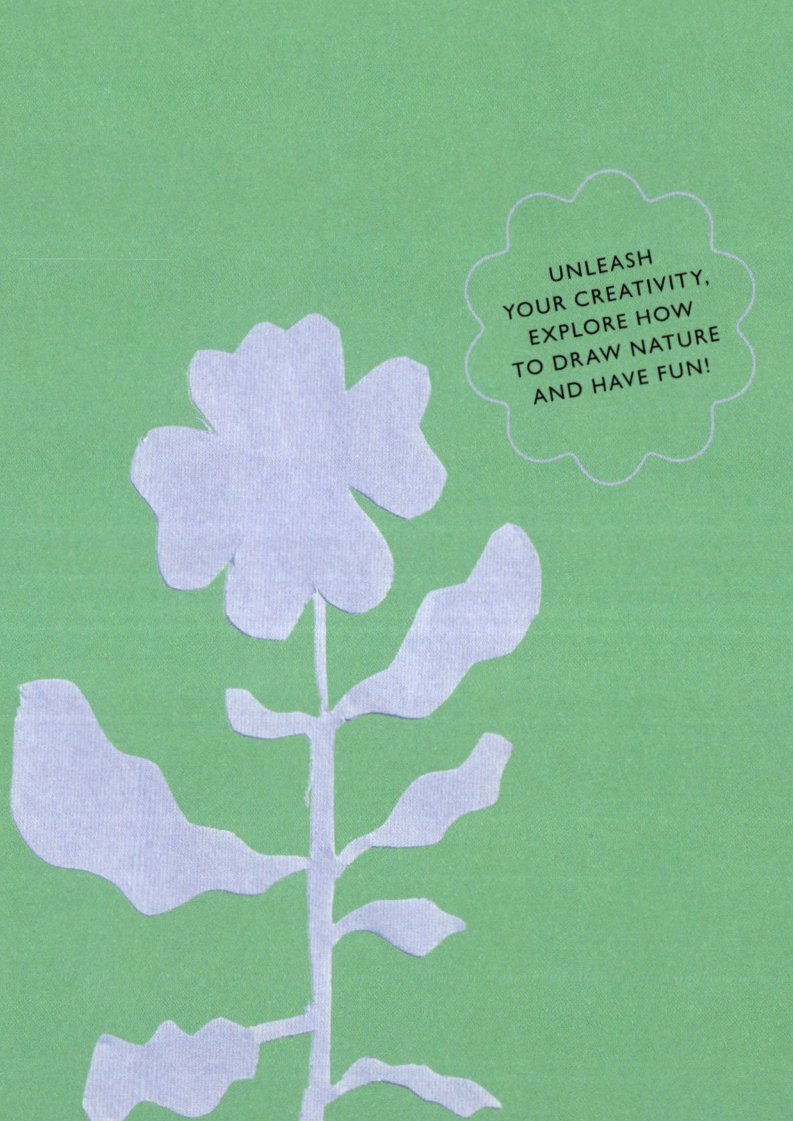
UNLEASH
YOUR CREATIVITY,
EXPLORE HOW
TO DRAW NATURE
AND HAVE FUN!

Contents

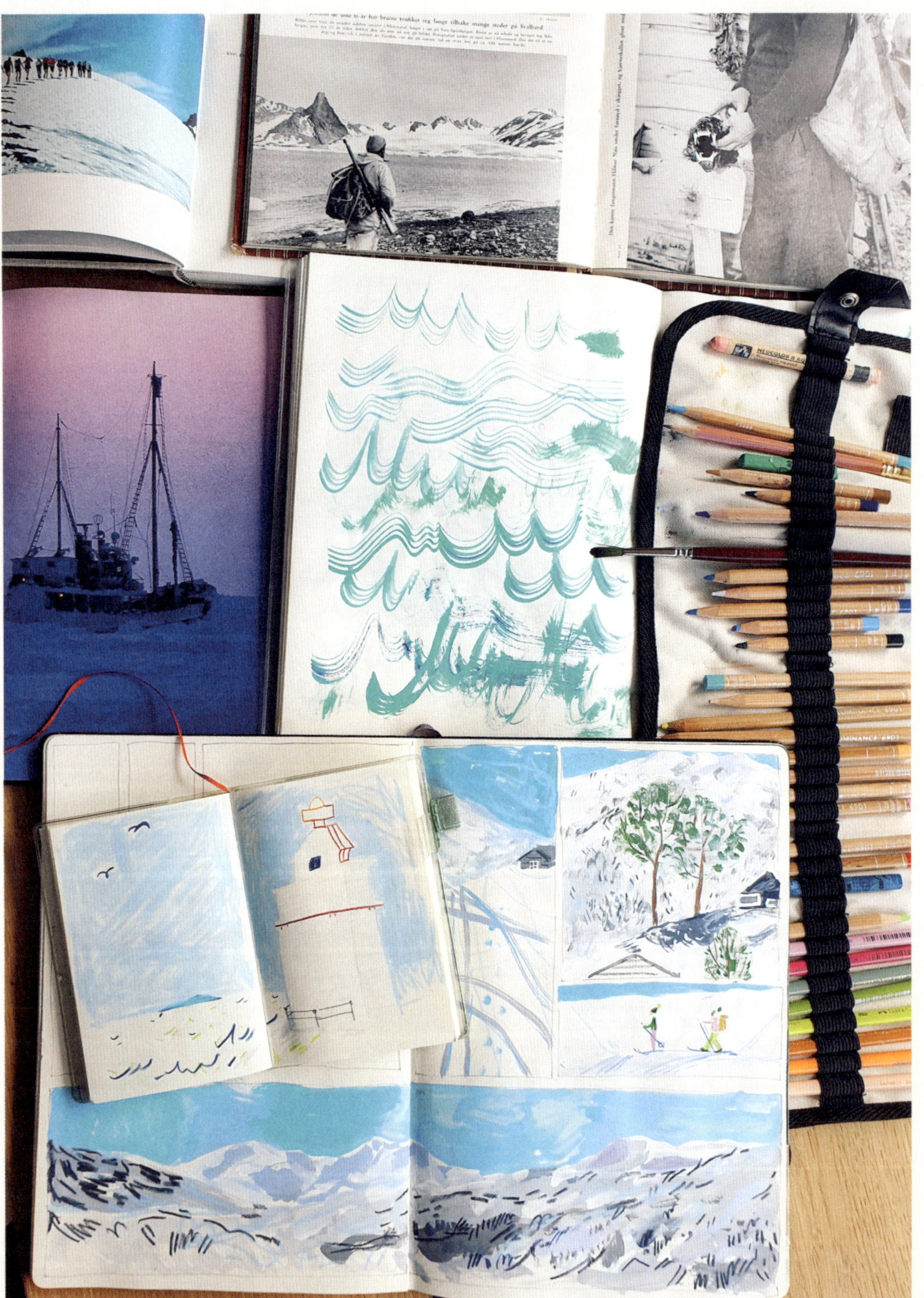

Introduction

WELCOME TO *DRAWING NATURE*

Hello and welcome to my third drawing book, a follow-up to the well-received *Drawing People, Drawing Nature.*

My name is Viktorija and I'm an illustrator and educator. My drawing classes vary from drawing people and nature, to gouache techniques, making zines and illustration. I have taught at the Victoria and Albert Museum in London, for Pinterest, at Art Highschool in Bergen, Norway, and many online classes both for creative professionals and hobby artists.

This book is a collection of creative prompts, playful exercises and sketches, based on years of teaching experience and observational drawing of nature.

I'll guide you from the basics of drawing to playing with composition, experimenting with materials, shifting your perspective and finding your voice when drawing nature. It is a diverse and playful book, helping you to navigate creativity, broaden your horizons and learn some fundamental rules along the way.

Whether you are someone who is just starting out or getting back into drawing, or someone who will draw in this book with your kids, or a creative professional in search of some play, welcome!

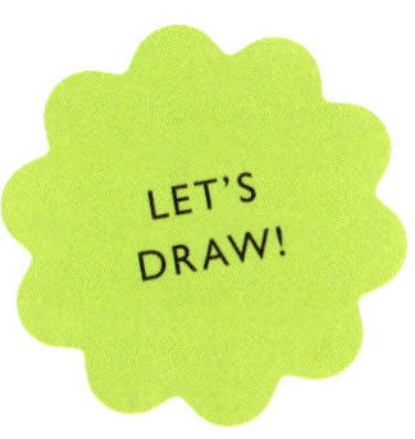

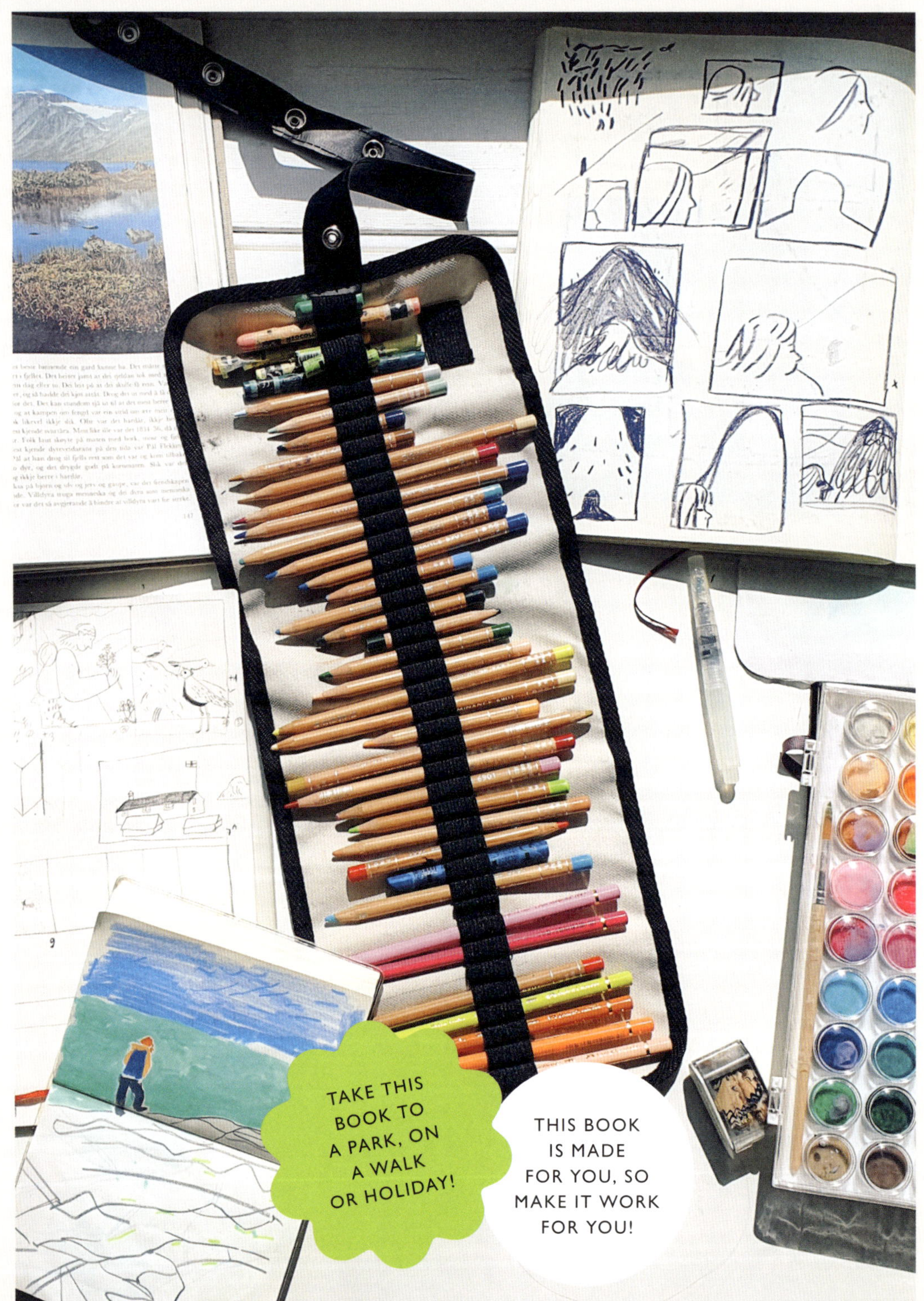
TAKE THIS BOOK TO A PARK, ON A WALK OR HOLIDAY!
THIS BOOK IS MADE FOR YOU, SO MAKE IT WORK FOR YOU!

How to Use This Book

PROJECT KEY:

PROJECT

PLAY

PROMPT

PROJECTS teach you how to draw by following an exercise along with Viktorija.

PLAYS are an opportunity to express yourself.

PROMPTS encourage you to try something new.

This book contains 100 projects on drawing nature that differ in difficulty and type. Some will focus on drawing techniques, others on composition and some will make you think outside the box!

Projects start with those that have more guidance and are fit for beginners. As you move through the book, the projects allow for more freedom and independence. You can either follow the projects sequentially or pick and choose any depending on the mood you're in and the time and materials you have to hand.

In some projects, you are advised to use techniques applicable to certain mediums. But it's just a suggestion. Get to know your materials, and understand their limitations and experiment, adjusting the exercise when you need to. Make it work for you.

If you would like, you can have a separate sketchbook dedicated to drawing nature, so you can extend the project briefs there, using it to test materials, create colour palettes or play with mark making.

Where you live will shape your drawings, so I encourage you to bring your surroundings into this book. Whether it's colours, patterns or drawing techniques! You may live in a place where you will have different types of trees, landscapes, flowers and animals. Make this book your own and adjust and change the prompts and plays where needed. You can use this book as a way to document your surroundings or gather holiday memories or dream places to visit – or a combination of all things!

Practice makes perfect! Treat drawing as you would any other new skill and do a little every day. You will soon see results!

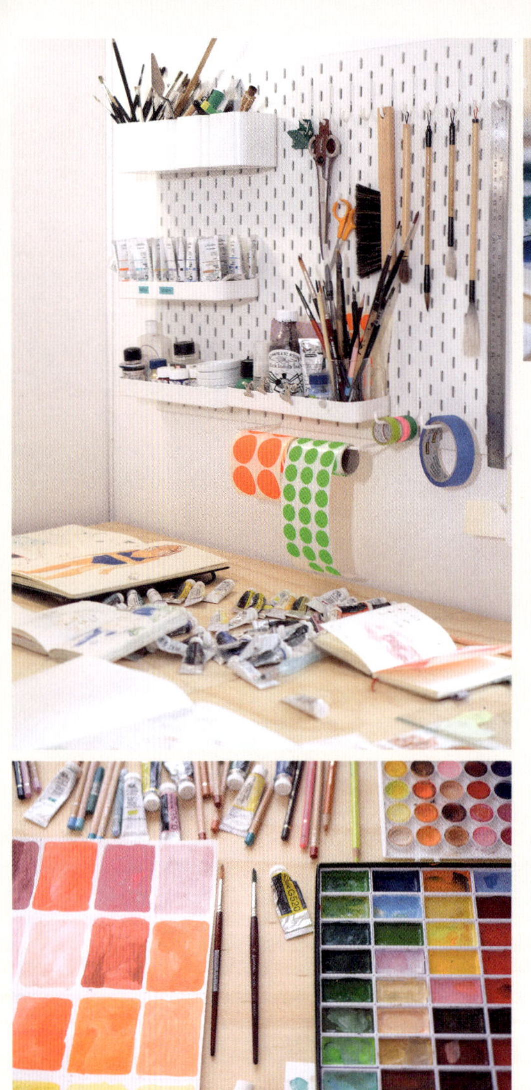

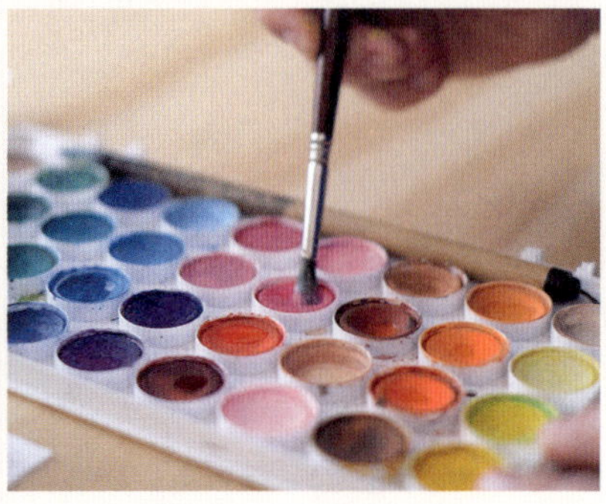

In this book I used different types of materials, ranging in both price and quality, from supermarket kids' gouache in pans to markers, pencils, pastels, ink and watercolours. I truly believe the best materials are the ones you already have and those you really enjoy using. Is it markers? Cheap watercolour paints? Expensive oil pencils? It's really up to you!

I love using art materials like children's gouache for shape and colouring pencils for lines. This is my favourite combination – something with a flowy quality and texture for shape and something that can achieve fun marks for the lines.

Aside from your medium of choice, you will need basic materials like a graphite pencil, eraser and pencil sharpener. In one of the projects, you will be encouraged to make a collage, so scissors and some tape or glue might be useful, too.

And how do you choose your preferred medium? I would recommend you think about these three things!

Tools & Materials

THIS BOOK DOESN'T REQUIRE ANY PARTICULAR TYPES OF MATERIALS – IT'S ALL ABOUT WHAT YOU ARE COMFORTABLE USING AS WELL AS MEDIUMS YOU WOULD LIKE TO EXPLORE.

1/ Line and shape.

When choosing mediums, think of using one type for making lines and another for creating shapes. For example, you can go for watercolours for shapes and pencils for lines. Or you can work with colouring pencils for both line and shape. The combinations are endless.

2/ Setting limitations is so important.

Narrowing down your materials will make the process more interesting for you. You can always switch up what you are using but first try using a limited selection of art materials.

3/ Working space.

Consider where you will be working. Will it be from your sofa, kitchen table or a designated desk? You can have a more elaborate set-up for some longer projects and a portable, on-the-go set-up for bite-size projects! Get a water brush if you want to use watercolours or gouache on the go, then you won't need a jar and a paintbrush. This will make the process so much easier.

You will be able to do all the projects in this book even with the most limited of materials. I am certain you will be able to complete the sketchbook and have fun with just one graphite pencil! It's all about having fun and enjoying the process, so no pressure.

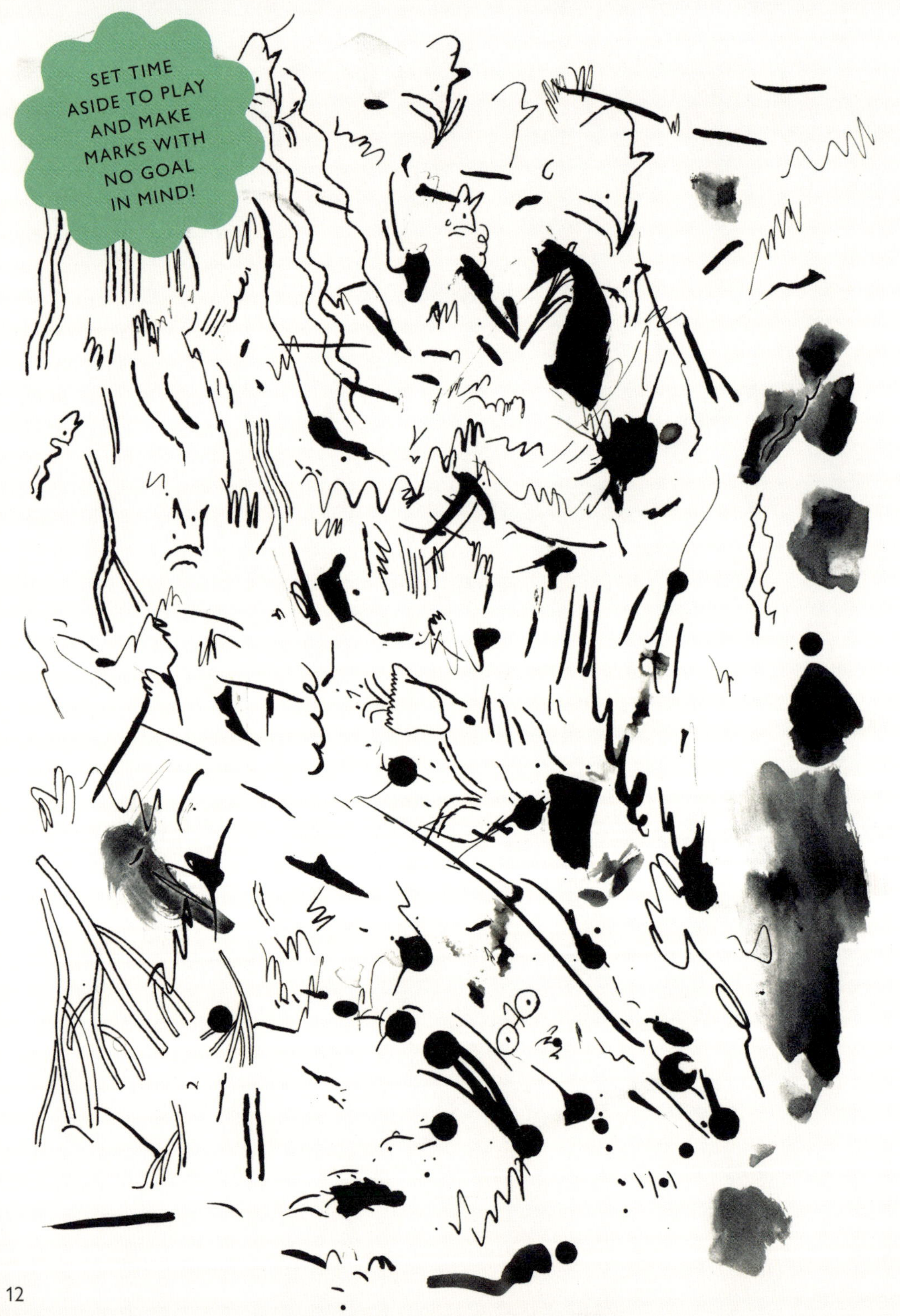
SET TIME ASIDE TO PLAY AND MAKE MARKS WITH NO GOAL IN MIND!

Mark Making

I LIKE TO THINK ABOUT MARKS IN THREE WAYS.

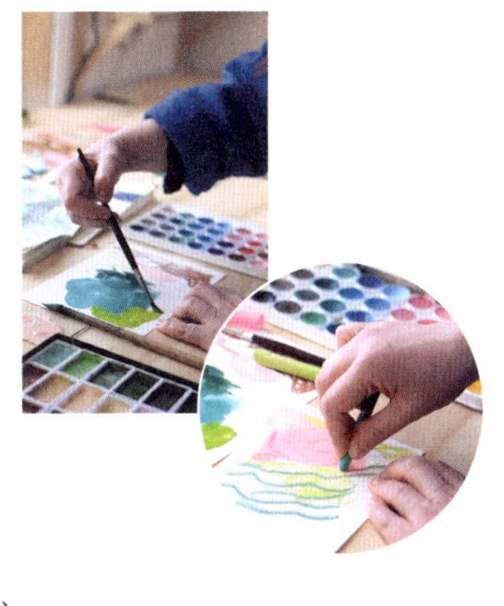

1/ The properties of the medium (whether its dry, powdery or water soluble).

What medium are you using? Can you add water to it, smear it or mix it? For example, if you are using a water-soluble pencil, try drawing directly on a wet surface as well as dipping the pencil in the water before drawing on dry paper to see what results you yield. If you are using markers, layer the different colours over each other, or use them to layer over the pencil. Examine the properties of each medium and don't be afraid to try something unexpected.

2/ How do you apply the medium to the paper?

How to make marks with your medium. For example, if you use a marker, try tapping it, creating dots or working really fast to cover an entire area. With a paintbrush, cover an area with an even layer of paint, make random brushstrokes or press the brush into the paper.

3/ How do you hold your painting tool?

When drawing with any tool, change the angle of how you hold it as well as the thickness of the line you make. Switch up the speed with which you make marks. Do you notice what kind of marks you are making if you are tense and slouched versus free and open? The marks you make will always reflect your feelings and body language.

Set time aside to play and make marks with no goal in mind! There are also unconventional methods, like using sticks to paint with ink to create unusual marks! Try to create your own library of marks that you can refer back to as you work, noticing which ones you enjoy making the most and those you are most curious to explore.

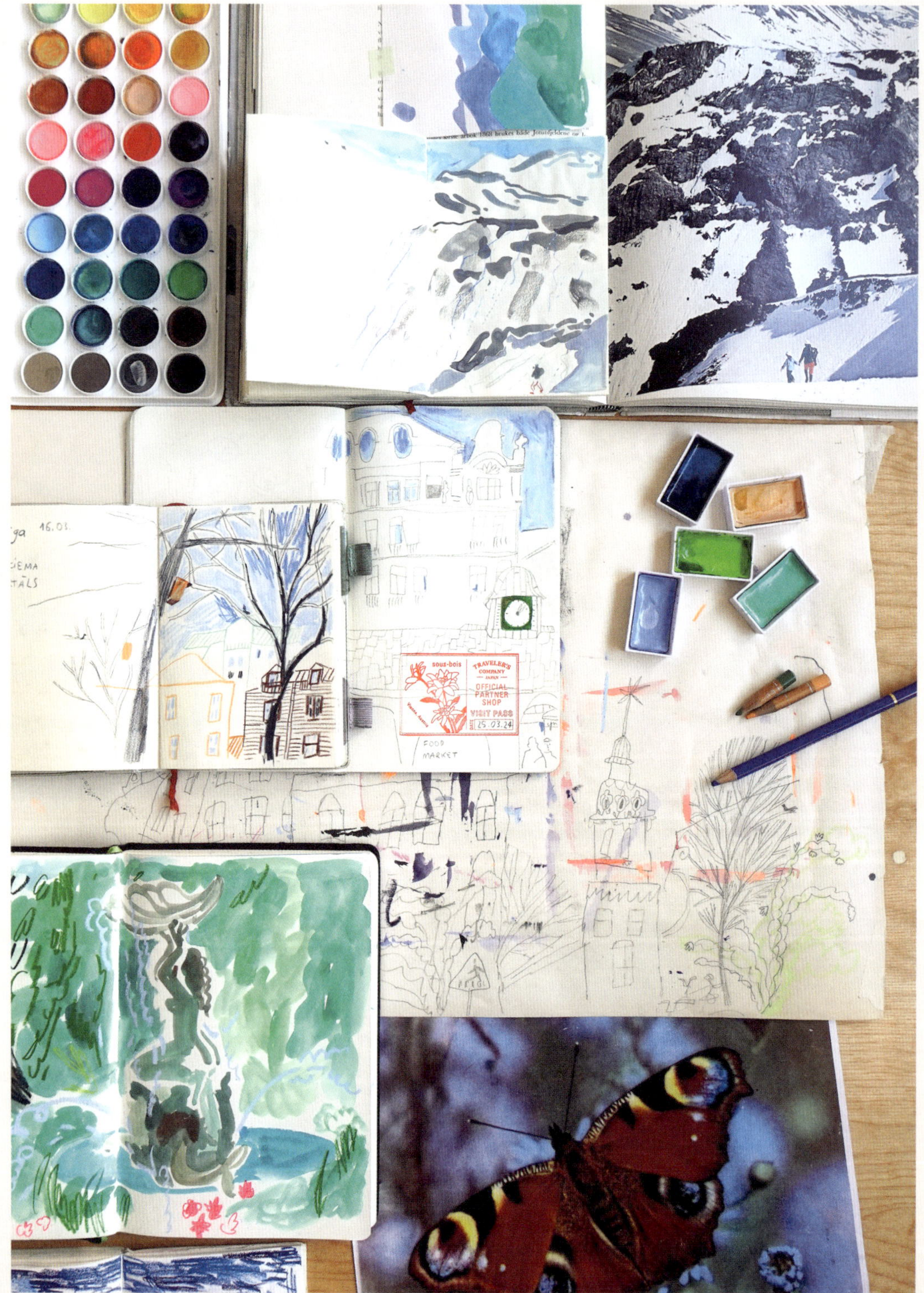
16.03.
sous-bois
TRAVELER'S COMPANY JAPAN
OFFICIAL PARTNER SHOP
VISIT PASS
25.03.24
FOOD MARKET

References & Observational DRAWING

IN SOME PROMPTS IN THIS BOOK YOU WILL BE ASKED TO COME UP WITH YOUR OWN MOTIF AND IDEA FOR THE PROMPT. SO HERE'S HOW TO FIND REFERENCES AND WHAT TO DO IF YOU DON'T LIVE NEXT TO NATURE.

Drawing from observation

This is the most exciting way to draw and it helps to develop your drawing skills in a different way than drawing from a photo. You hear all the sounds on location, plus you can look up, down, left, right – you can even walk around the object you are drawing. You can really look closely and observe the movement, colour and change of light.

Remember that all nature is nature. No matter if it's a weed on the pavement, potted herbs in your kitchen, a houseplant, a view from a window, a flower-bed, nature reserve or forest.

Sketch down some nature elements when you are on your commute to work or waiting for a bus and then use your sketches to work in the book.

Photo references

Using photo references is a great way to find inspiration. But be mindful of several things: when you use photo reference a lot of creative decisions were already made, like the composition, subject, position and angle.

Vintage books also provide an incredible variety of great photo references for nature. From animal encyclopedias to botanical books with photos of plants, to geological, geographical and other titles, as well as adventure books, national park guides and more. If you want you can also search the internet for a picture – it's ok to do so just for your own enjoyment. A close-up of a leaf, butterfly or a scene from a faraway land.

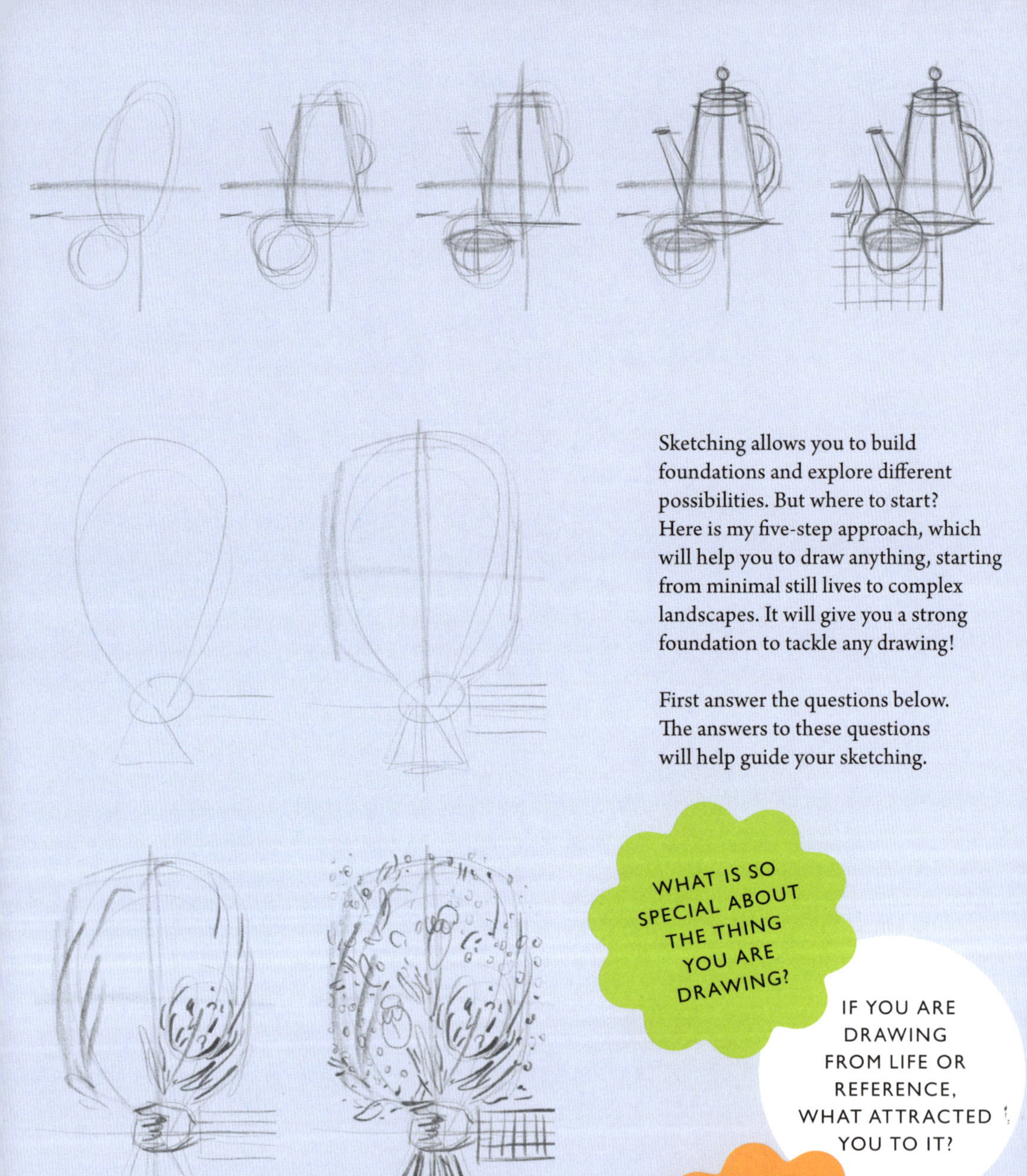

Sketching allows you to build foundations and explore different possibilities. But where to start? Here is my five-step approach, which will help you to draw anything, starting from minimal still lives to complex landscapes. It will give you a strong foundation to tackle any drawing!

First answer the questions below. The answers to these questions will help guide your sketching.

WHAT IS SO SPECIAL ABOUT THE THING YOU ARE DRAWING?

IF YOU ARE DRAWING FROM LIFE OR REFERENCE, WHAT ATTRACTED YOU TO IT?

AND WHAT ARE YOU TRYING TO COMMUNICATE?

THE FIVE-STEP APPROACH TO DRAWING ANYTHING AND EVERYTHING.

Here is how to start and build up your drawing. The same approach can be applied to drawing still lives, landscapes, portraits, drawing from your imagination and pretty much anything else, including abstract work.

Start sketching loose and fast. To help you loosen up, hold your pencil closer to the end (further away from the sharp tip). As you progress with your sketch and add more details, you will naturally hold your pencil tighter and lower to give you more control over it. Think of your sketch as a whole, especially in the first few steps. Work on all parts of the drawing equally as you go.

1. Start with light and loose pencil marks. Big areas first. Sketch rough areas in geometric shapes in very light and loose lines. Usually one to four zones is enough to mark where things will be and get an idea of your composition.

2. Geometric shapes. Sketch more details and add more areas using loose and light lines and geometric shapes but don't invest. Develop your sketch equally as you go and pay attention to all aspects of the drawing before adding details. It's easy to move around and erase objects and shapes at this stage. Now is a good time to channel some energy and motion into your drawing. You can skew objects or create a direction to create a more interesting and dynamic composition.

3. Guidelines channel energy and motion, allowing you to move, adjust and give direction to your initial sketch. For whatever object you are drawing add vertical and horizontal guidelines to the middle. This will help you to get the proportions right. Compare your objects to each other in terms of height and width. Look at a drawing as a whole.

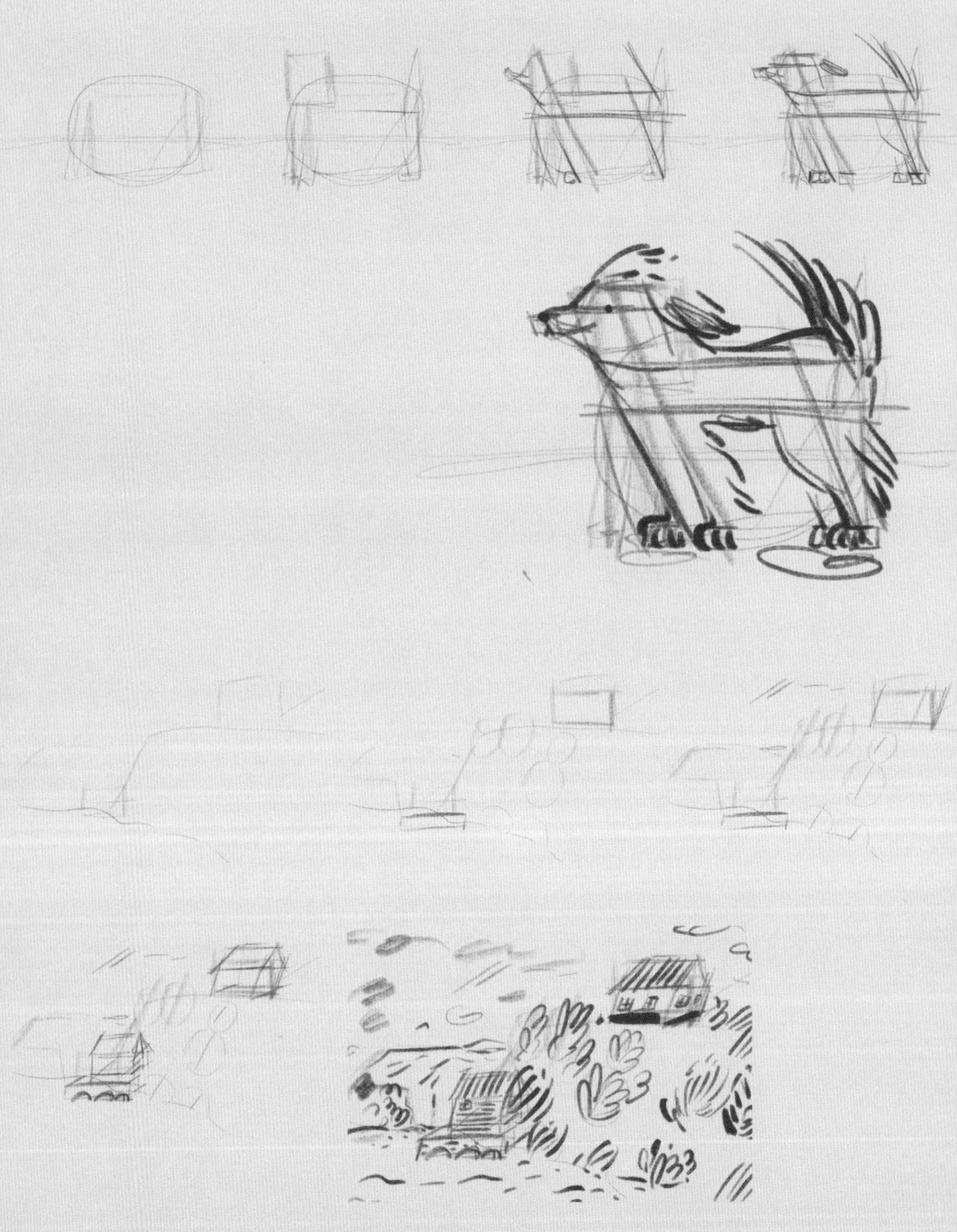

4. Geometric shapes in 3D. At this point start thinking about composition as a three-dimensional space, so if it was a square it will become a cube and shapes will start to have context. Add depth as well as height and width and place the objects and shapes in order of perspective and ground them. By doing these things you will add some depth and dimension to your drawing.

5. Add details and textures. Okay, so you have drawn your rough composition, added your geometric shapes and guidelines, and made them into 3D objects. We now move on to adding details in the same way as before: we view elements as shapes. Add as many details as you like to the drawing but work on all parts of the composition equally. At this point add loose and organic marks and other details to create a more finished sketch ready to be painted.

It doesn't matter if your drawing is very stylised and flat or if you are going for a realistic look; this approach is a good point to start to help you place objects and play around with composition.

Be mindful that your sketch is made of lines and if you choose to finish it off with a different medium, it will also have colours, shapes and marks. It will look very different when painted.

To figure out your drawing and composition, I would recommend you start with drawing small thumbnails. Thumbnails are an excellent way of experimenting with different compositions. Draw a few thumbnails in the same proportions as your planned drawing no bigger than 4 cm (1½ in) tall. Fill them in with different compositions of whatever you are drawing. Choose the one which works even at this small scale. Even when you are drawing from real life or when on location, draw a quick thumbnail to figure out the composition and use it as a guideline later for your final drawing or painting.

Remember that if you want to loosen your drawing, change how you hold the pencil and hold it further away from the sharp end. Be mindful if you are drawing just with your hand or your arm and your body is moving too. Experiment with doing different things and whole arm and body motions.

Change the size you are drawing on. If you usually draw on A6 or A5 size paper, change up for an A2 sheet. Buy cheap newsprint and go big and wild!

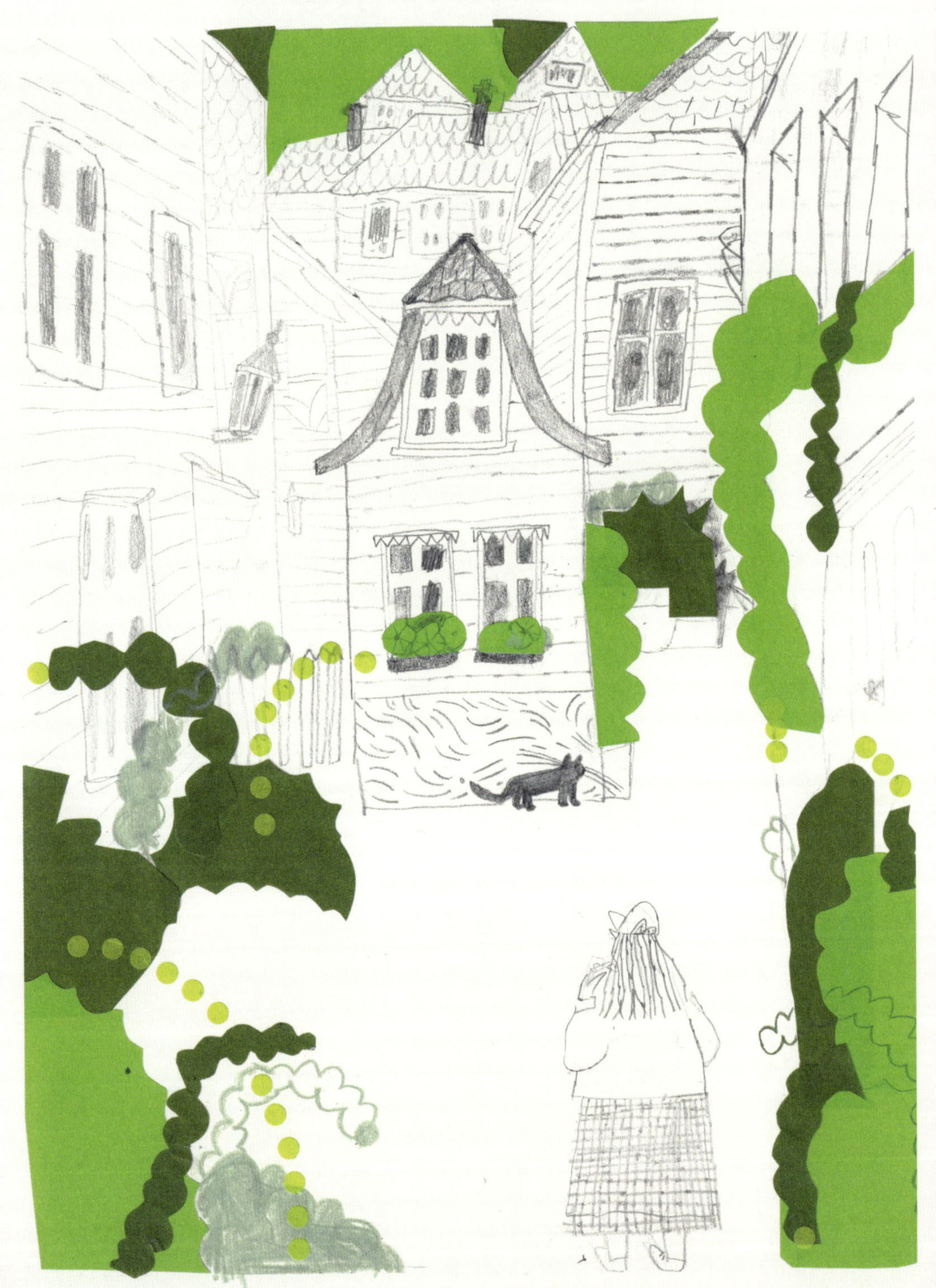

Making a Picture

LINE + SHAPE + COLOUR + MARK MAKING

How many times have you heard people call someone talented at drawing? As if it's an inherited skill which you either have or don't. At other times drawing can be seen as akin to some sort of magic, which you can intuitively channel to achieve a great drawing. Luckily, none of these things are true. Drawing and creativity are skills and work more like a muscle: the more you train them, the stronger and better they get. And doing the right exercises and having the right structure may not make us a great artist, but it will allow us to make good pictures.

We all have our own way of drawing, which can be dictated by the medium we are using, our style, the subject or the way that we make marks. All of us lean towards some of these more than others and we can combine them to achieve the desired result. The combination and variations are endless. Look at your favourite artists and illustrators' work and you should easily be able to tell which of these qualities dominate their artwork. Which types do you use most in your work?

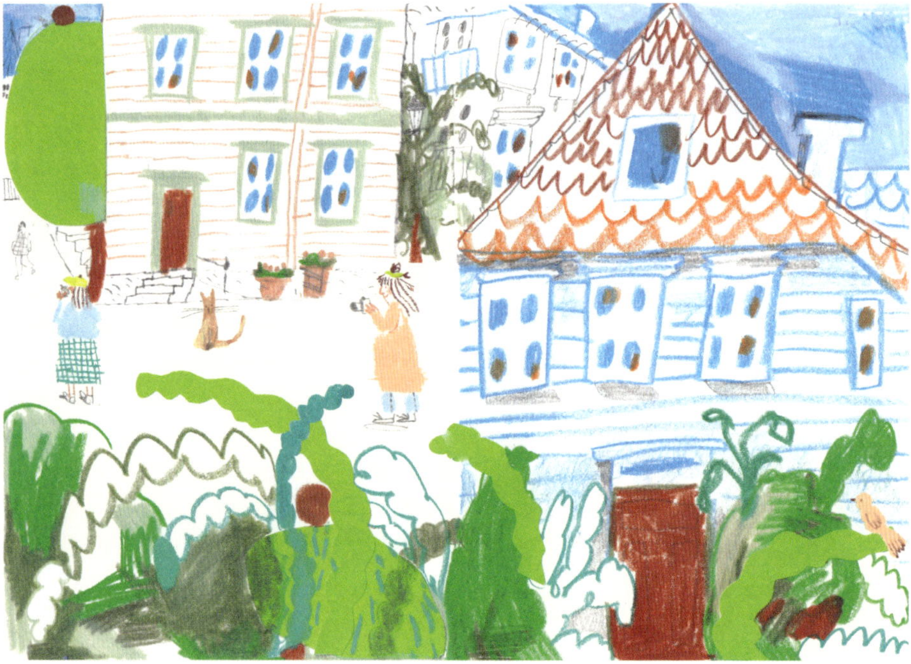

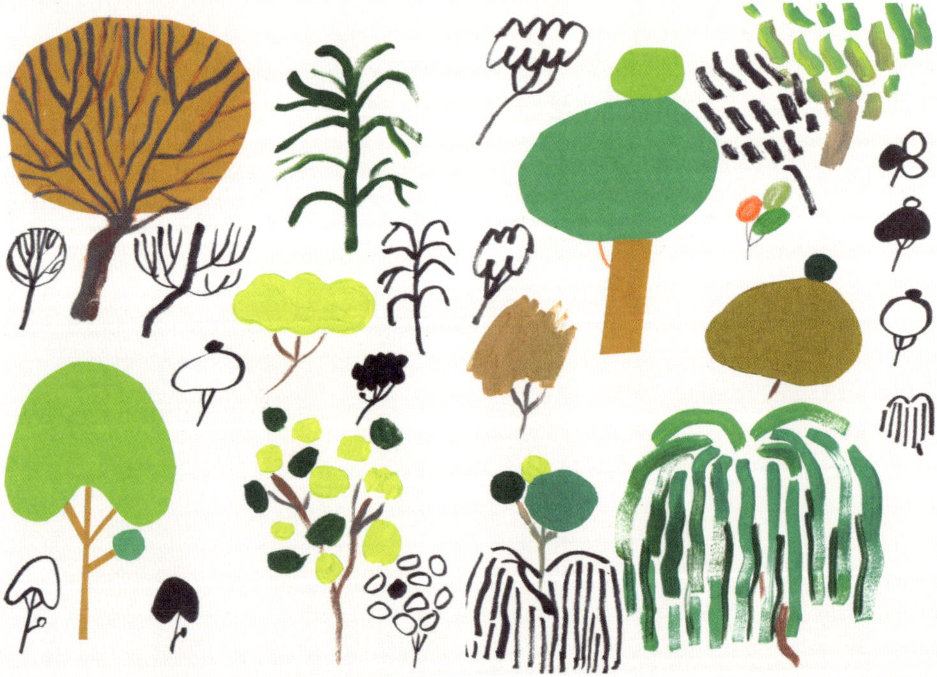

THINGS TO CONSIDER WHEN YOU ARE DRAWING.

You don't have to make pretty pictures. And each drawing can have a different goal. One is an experiment and play, next one is an observational drawing of your surroundings, a third one is a graphic piece for your kitchen wall.

Composition is one of the most fun things to play with. What are you trying to communicate? Is your subject small and delicate or large and intimidating? Is there a confident or playful mood? If you draw an object that fills your page, it will come across as dominating and large. Cut your object off and have it peeking onto a page and notice how this changes the drawing.

Changing the **angle and viewpoint** will add an interesting visual element to your picture, help to highlight your subject, frame the detail or tell a story.

Exaggerating the drawing and skewing objects will add a dynamic aspect, some movement and a story. Elongate the flower stems, distort familiar objects and change proportion to communicate your end goal.

SET YOUR INTENTION AND GET READY TO ENJOY YOUR ART.

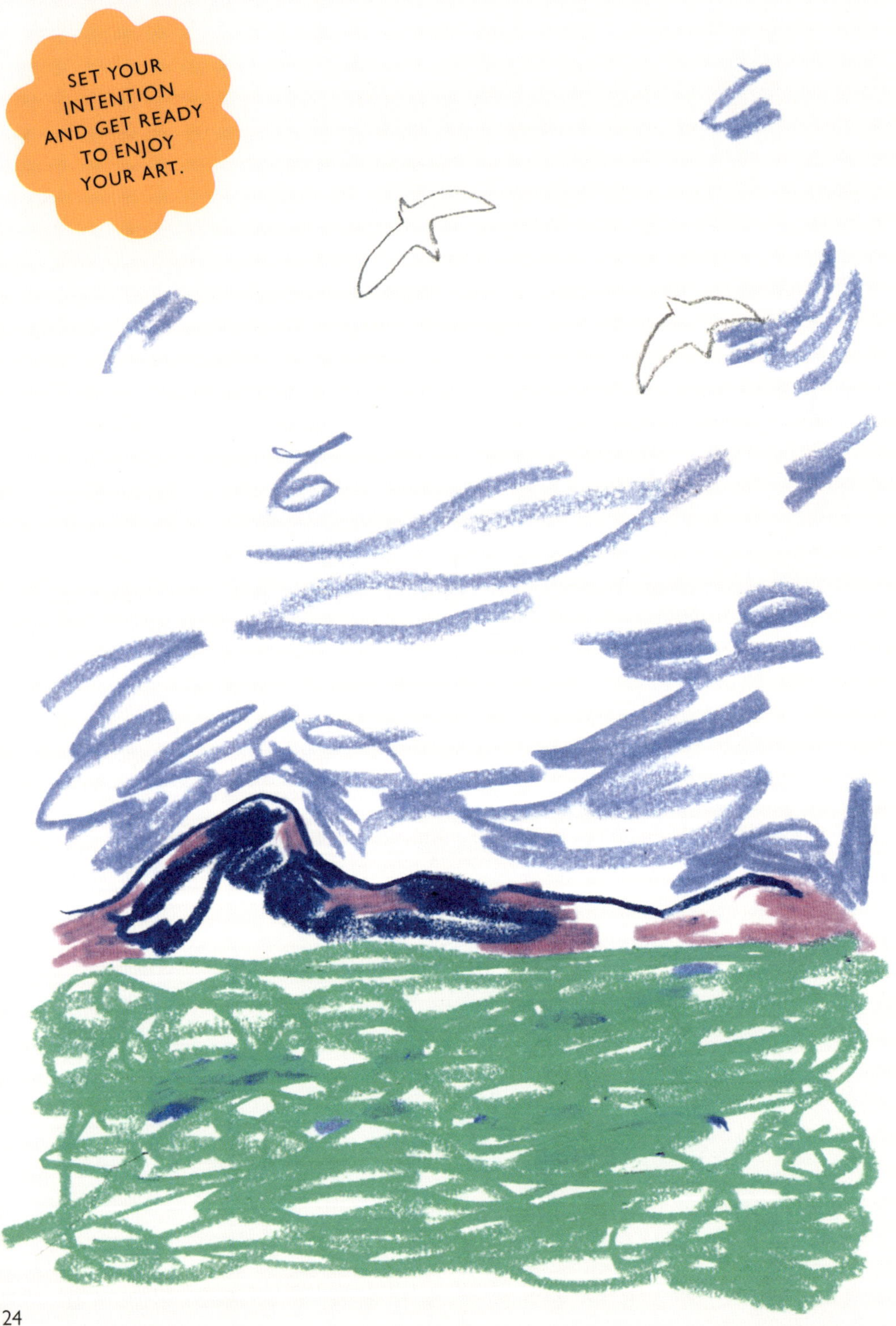

Intention

WRITE A MESSAGE FOR YOURSELF, A PHRASE TO INSPIRE YOUR DRAWINGS AND SET THE TONE FOR THE BOOK.

Is it a nudge to stop and look around, to be present, to ground yourself with drawing? Or to find your style, to make a journal documenting your surroundings? For me it's about noticing fleeting moments of nature, to enjoy the mundane! Think about it and create a friendly reminder for yourself!

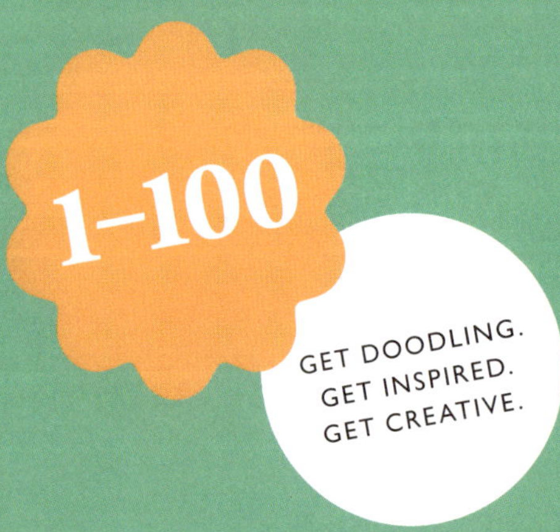
1–100
GET DOODLING.
GET INSPIRED.
GET CREATIVE.

The Exercises

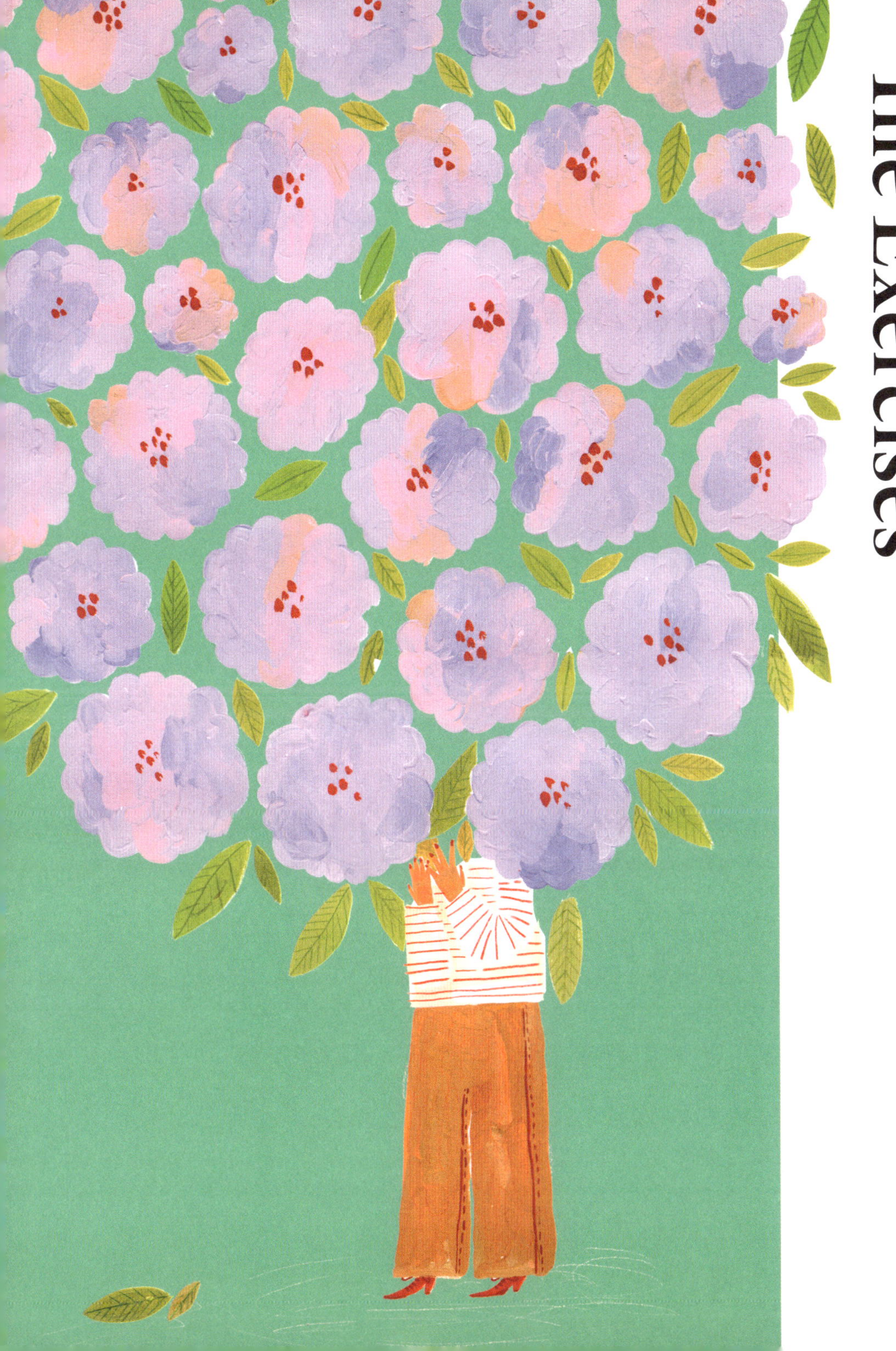

HOW WE REMEMBER THINGS DIFFERS GREATLY FROM WHAT THINGS ACTUALLY LOOK LIKE.

In these exercises, try to draw from reference rather than from memory. Collect some flowers and foliage while out walking, seek inspiration from a gardening or botanical book or search for examples online. Starting with leaves, notice the different shapes and colours, then try to draw as much variety as possible!

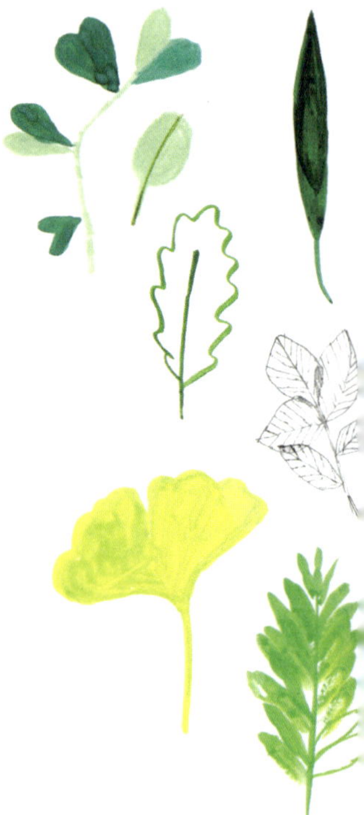

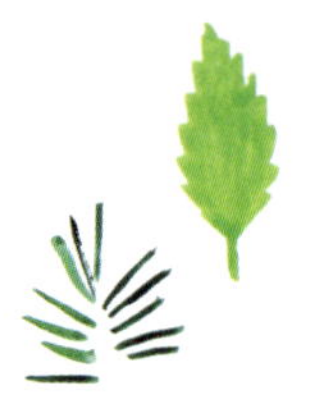

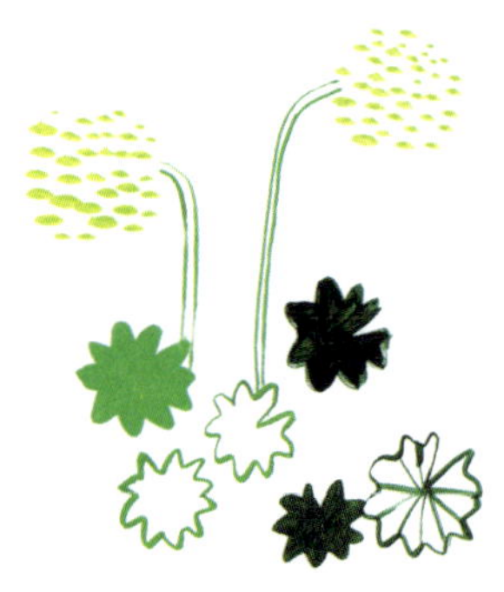

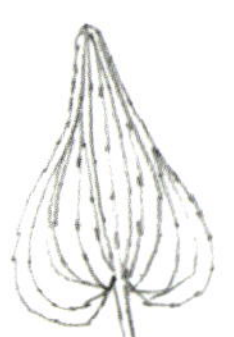

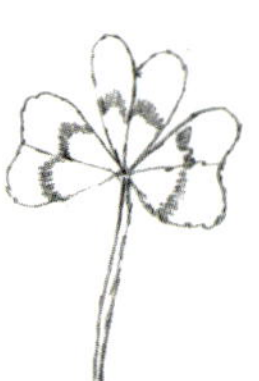

NOW HAVE A GO AT DRAWING FLOWERS.

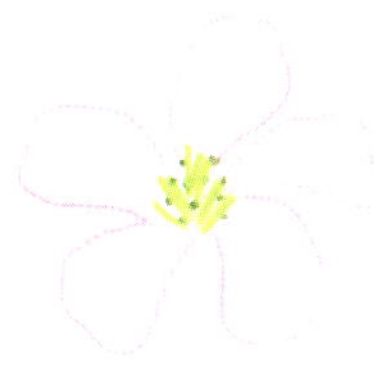

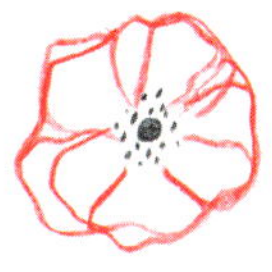

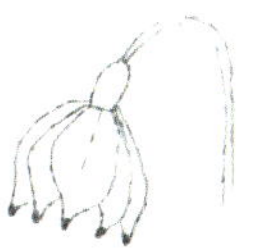

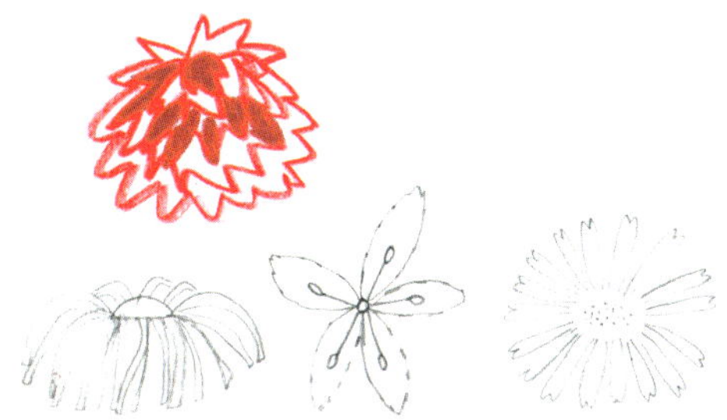

DRAW DIFFERENT FRUITS, VEGETABLES AND BERRIES, AND FILL IN THE PAGES WITH AS MANY DIFFERENT SHAPES, SIZES AND TEXTURES AS YOU CAN.

Think about playful mark making and colour!

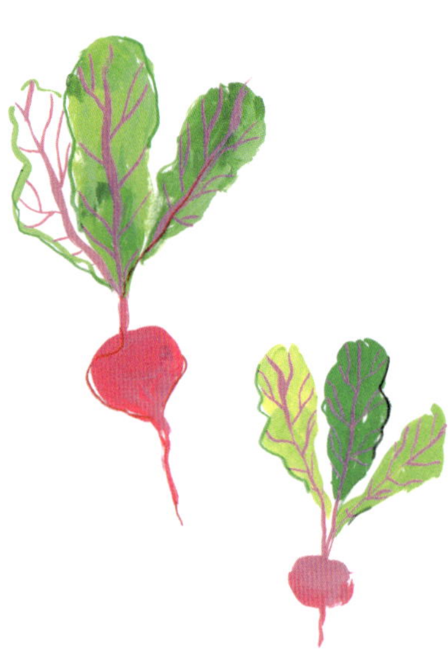

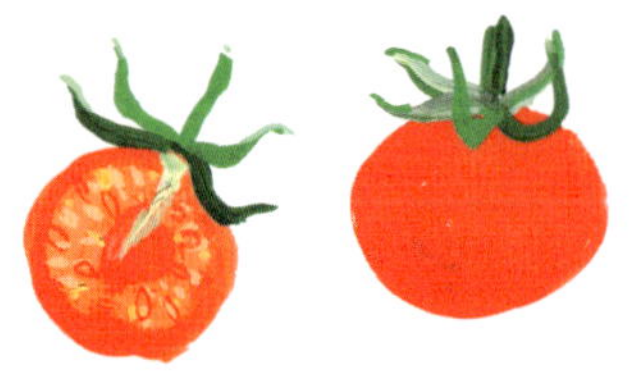

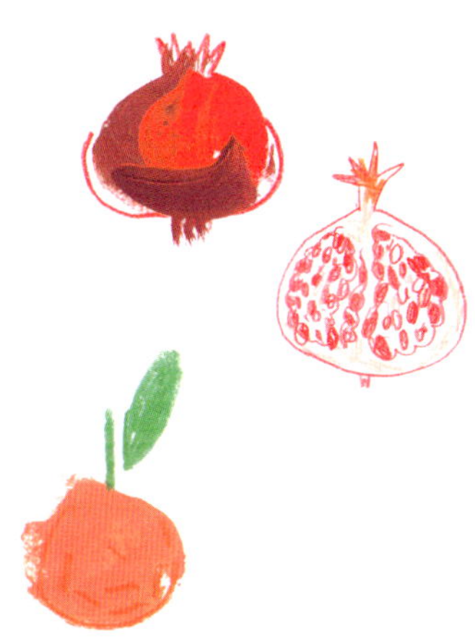

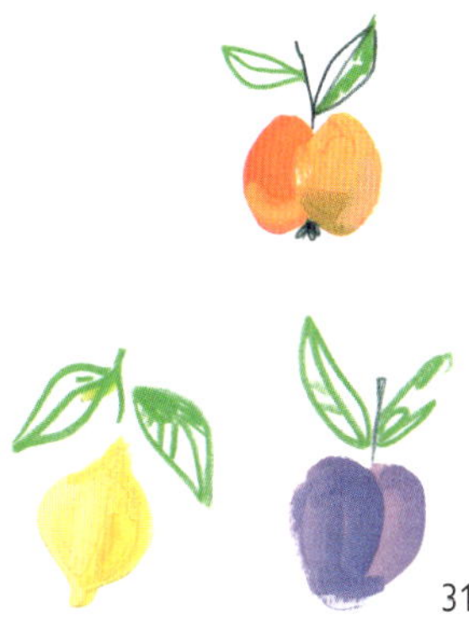

DRAW A BOUQUET OF FLOWERS IN THIS LADY'S HANDS.

Use different colours, textures and patterns to create a wide variety of blooms.

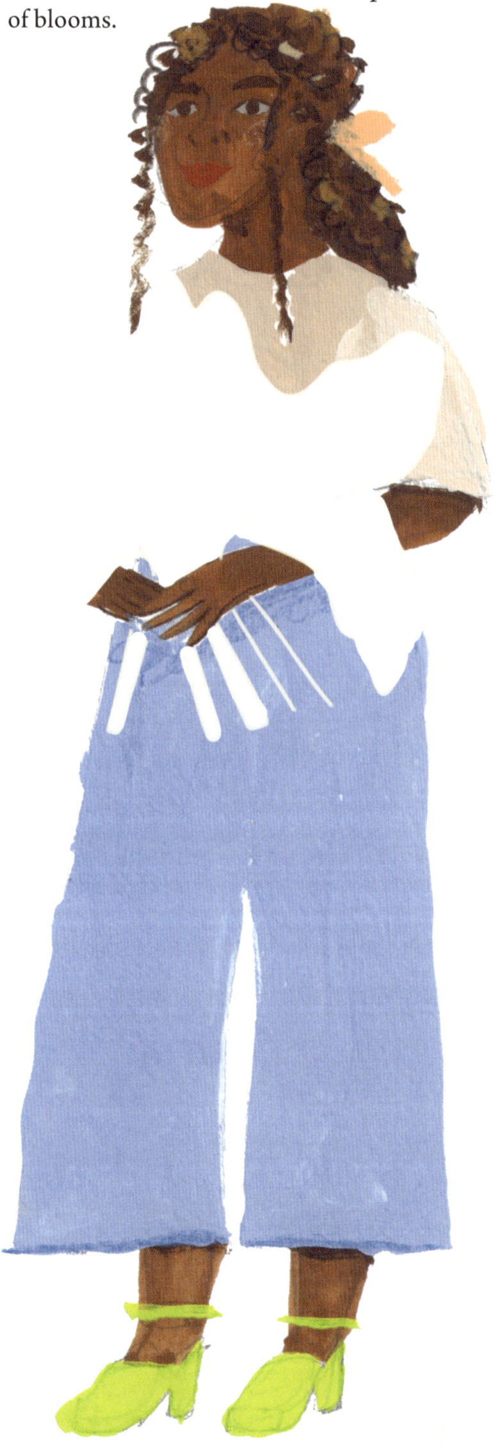

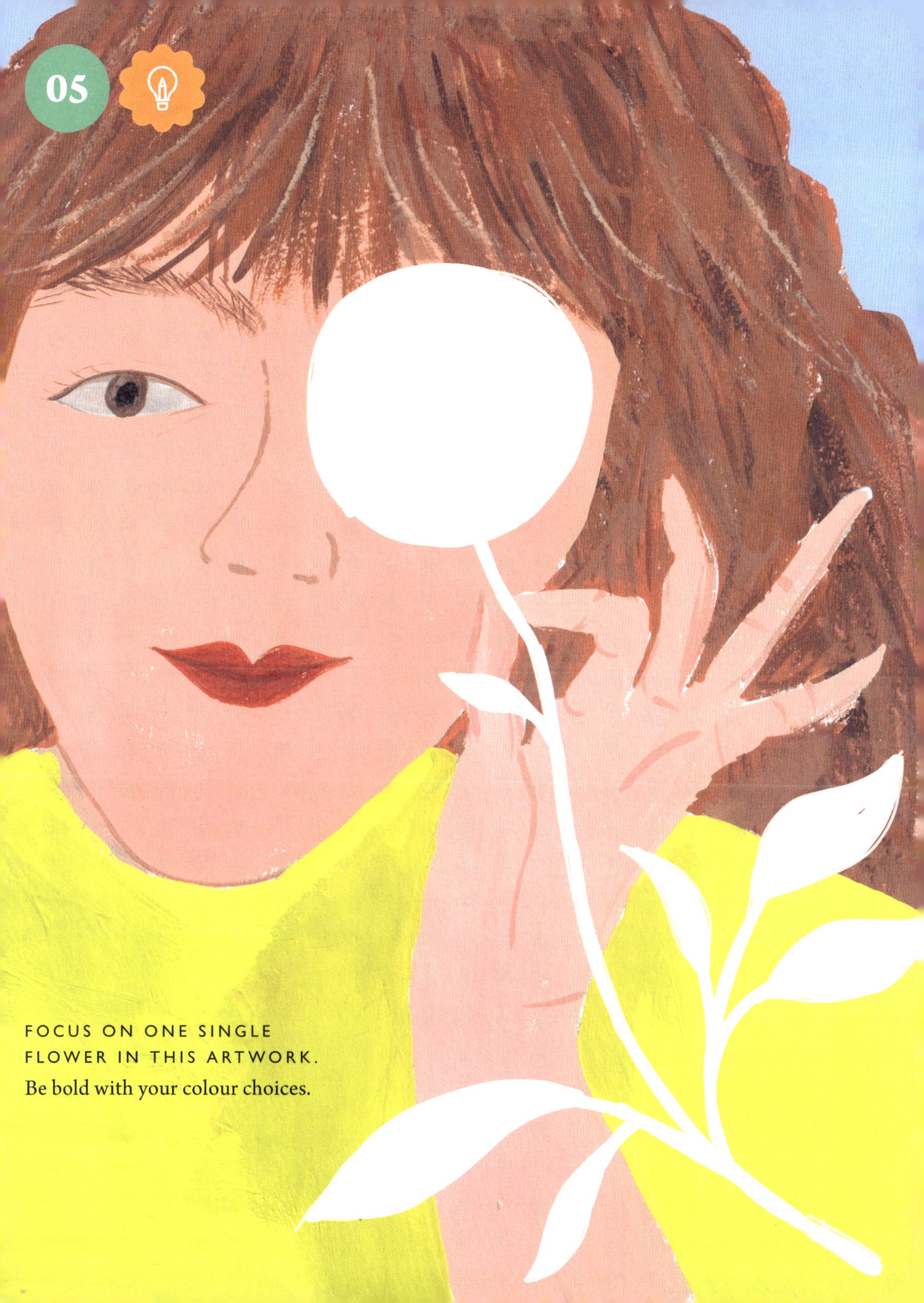
05
FOCUS ON ONE SINGLE
FLOWER IN THIS ARTWORK.
Be bold with your colour choices.

DRAW SOME FLOWERS THAT ARE COMMON WHERE YOU LIVE.

For me it is forget-me-nots, daffodils and pansies. Fill the page, experimenting with using just line, full colour and playful mark making.

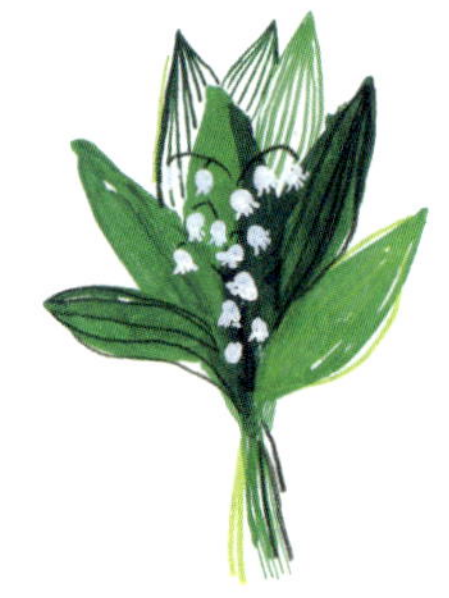

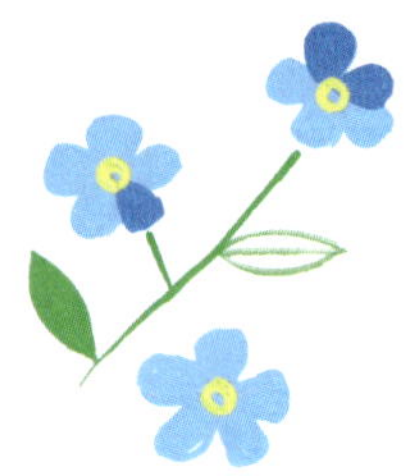

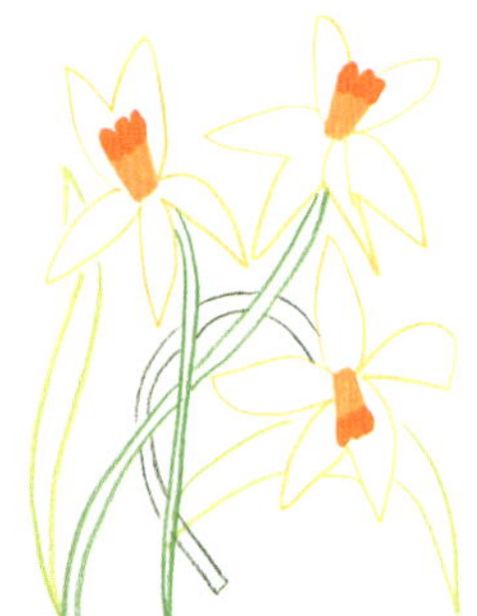

WHEN DRAWING A FLORAL BOUQUET, WE OFTEN START WITH THE FLOWERS, ADDING LEAVES AROUND EACH BLOOM.

This time, let's start the other way round. Colour in the greenery – adding texture and cute details – and leave the flowers until last.

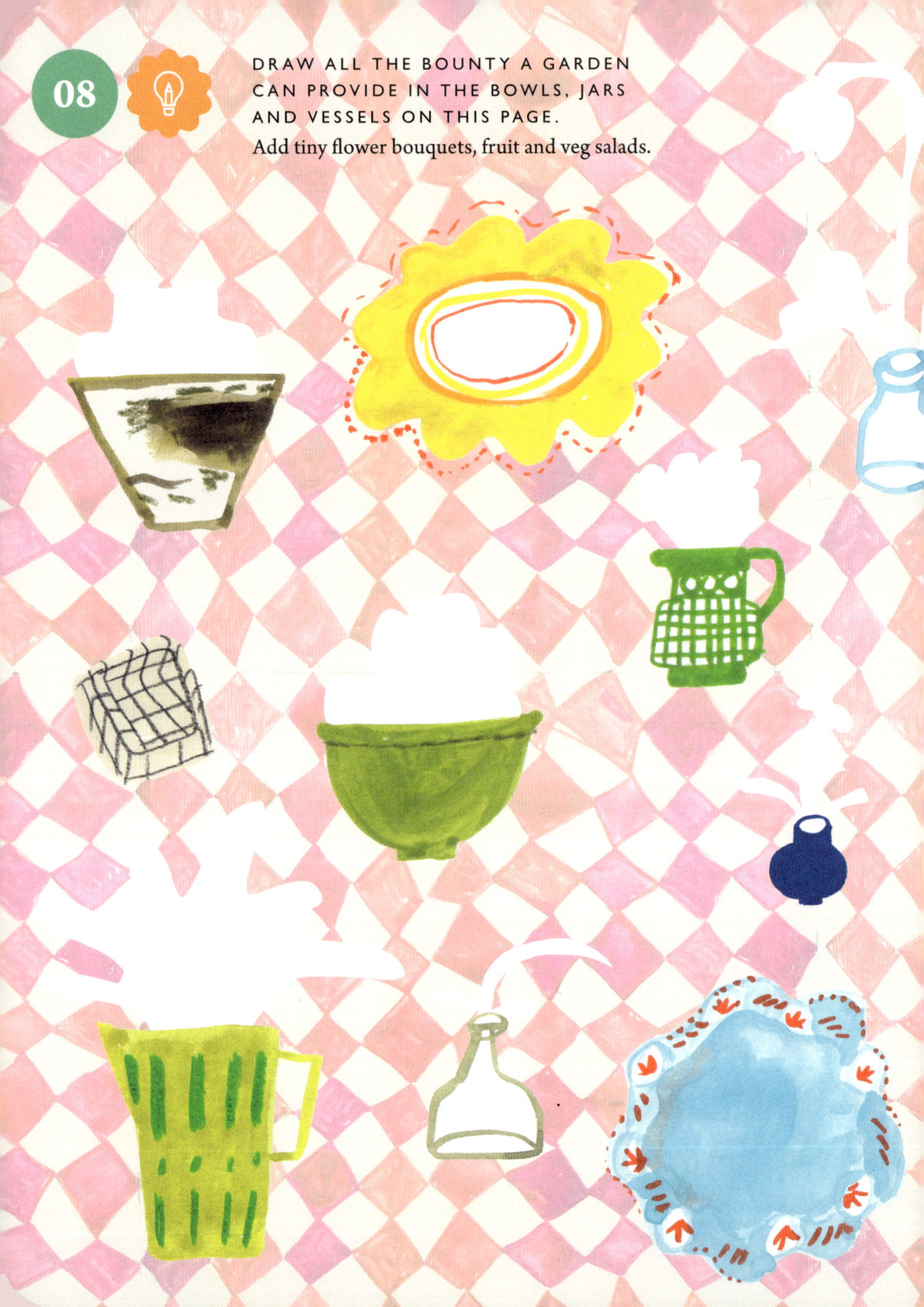
08
DRAW ALL THE BOUNTY A GARDEN CAN PROVIDE IN THE BOWLS, JARS AND VESSELS ON THIS PAGE.
Add tiny flower bouquets, fruit and veg salads.

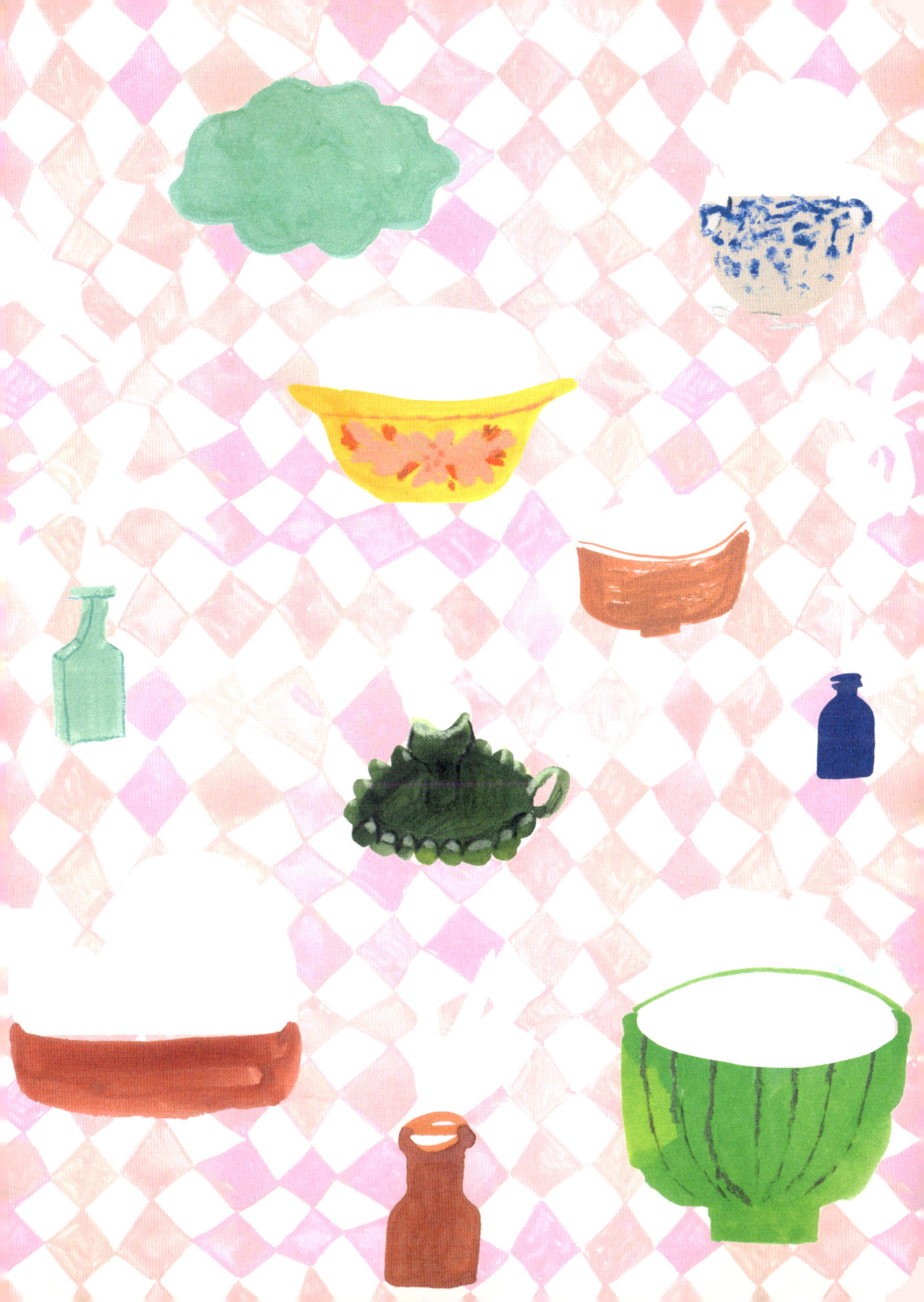

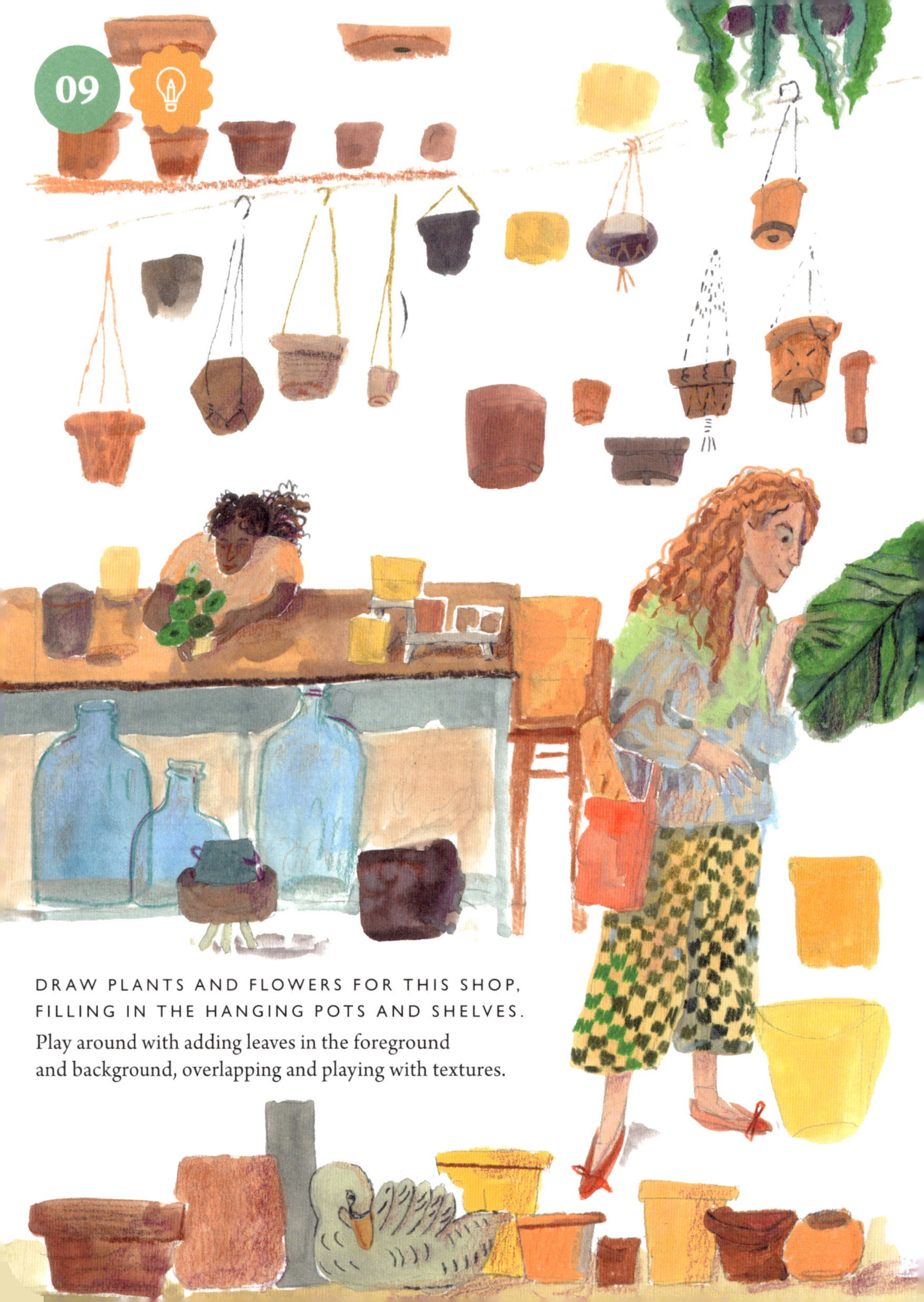

DRAW PLANTS AND FLOWERS FOR THIS SHOP, FILLING IN THE HANGING POTS AND SHELVES.

Play around with adding leaves in the foreground and background, overlapping and playing with textures.

DRAW A CLOSE-UP OF A HOUSEPLANT, PLAYING AROUND WITH SHAPES, LINES AND MARK MAKING!

Fill the whole page.

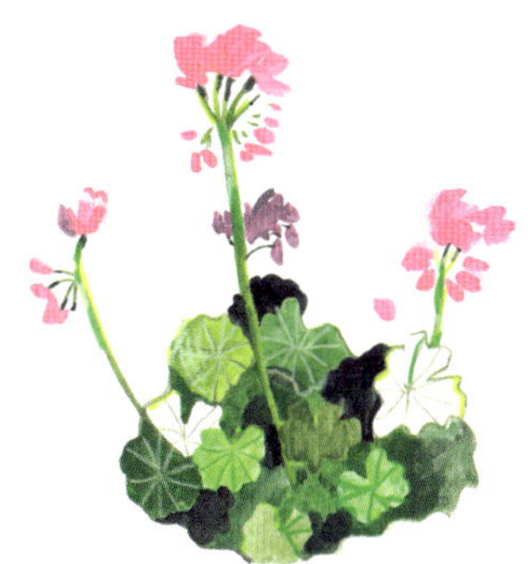

11

USING ONE COLOURING PENCIL (OR MARKER OR PEN), ADD LINES, PATTERNS AND MARKS TO THESE ABSTRACT SHAPES.

What do you see in each? A flower? A dog? A river?

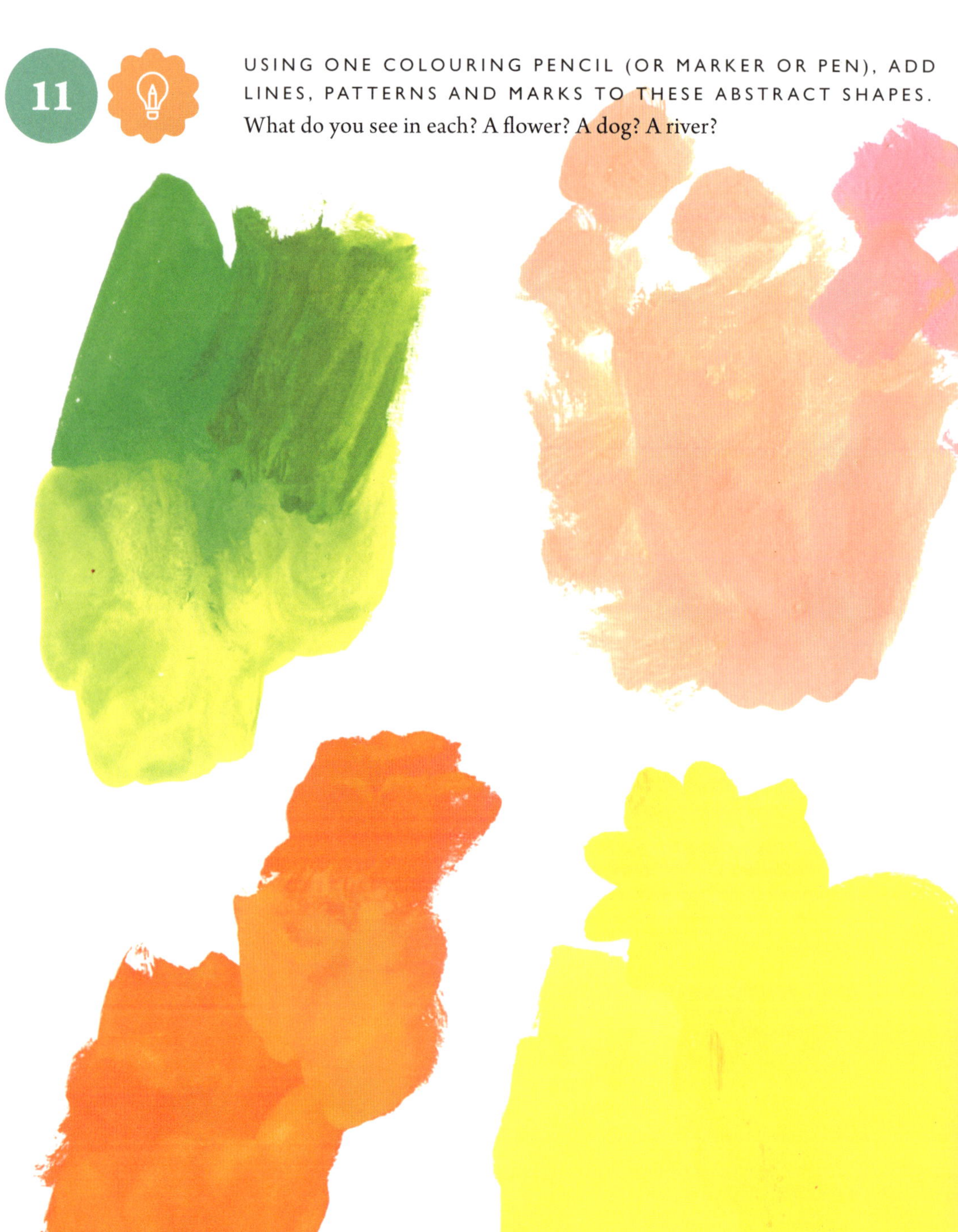

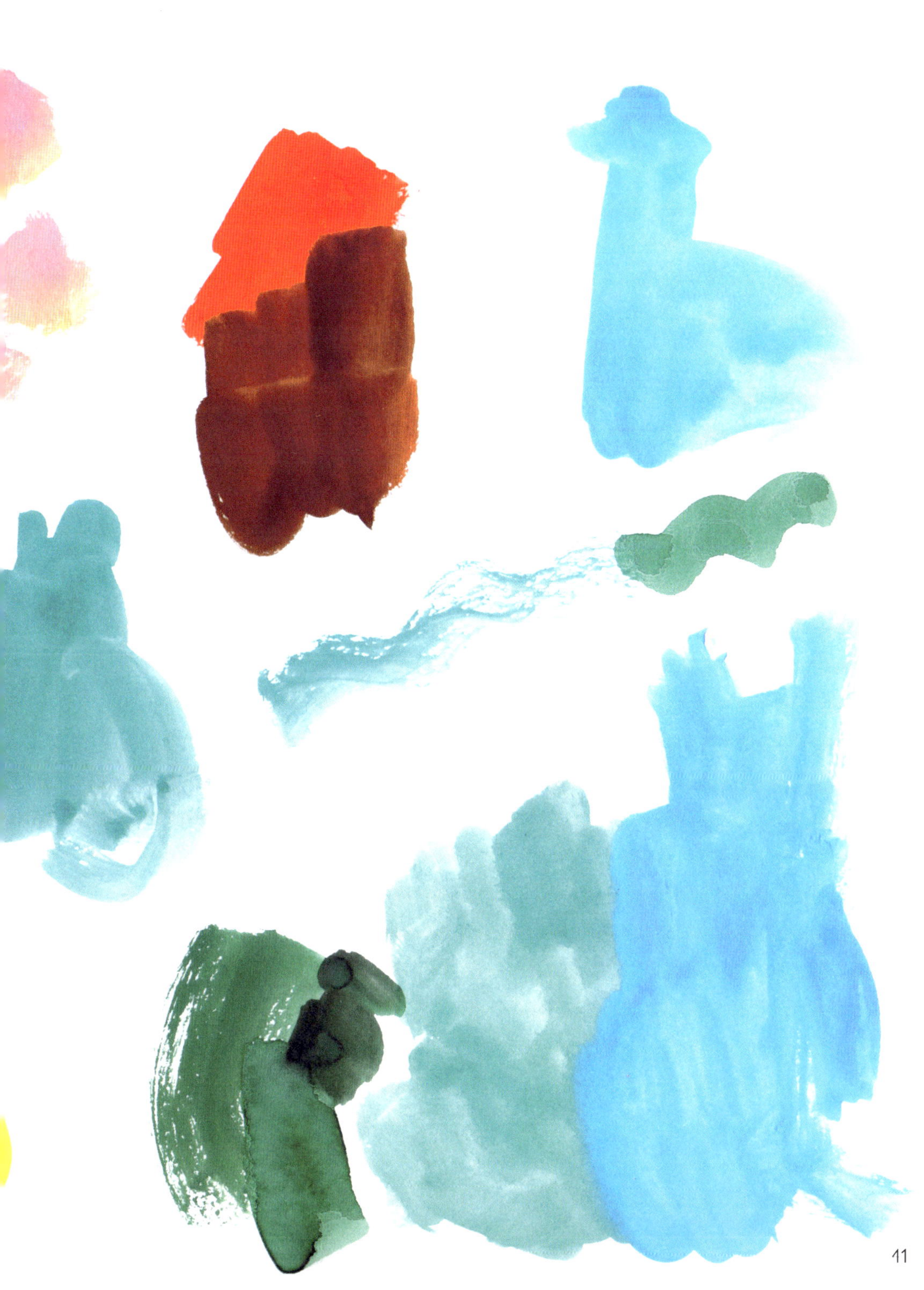

DRAW THE INSECTS THAT THIS CHILD IS HUNTING FOR, FOLLOWING THE GUIDELINES.

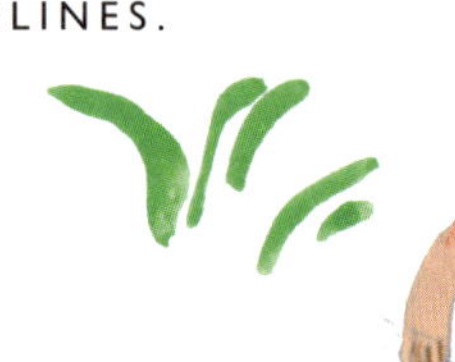

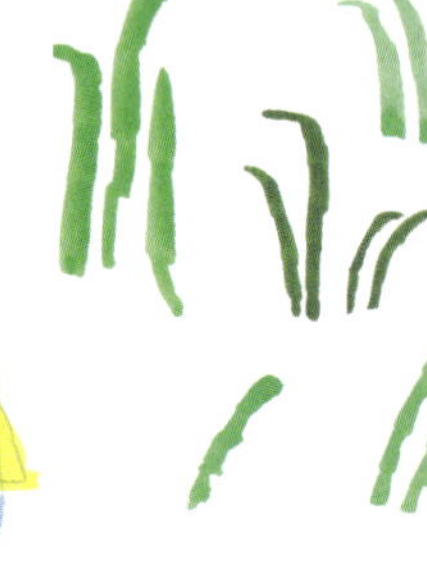

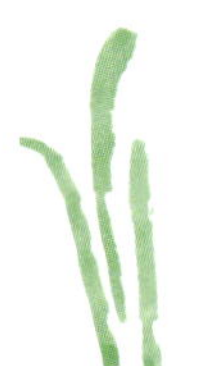

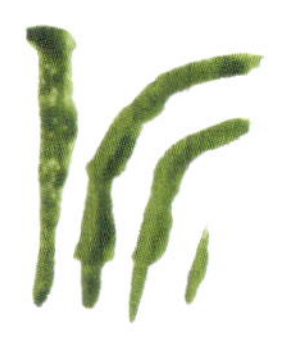

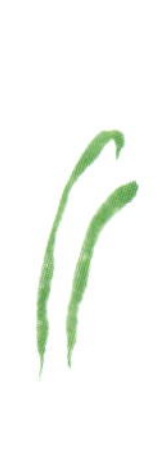

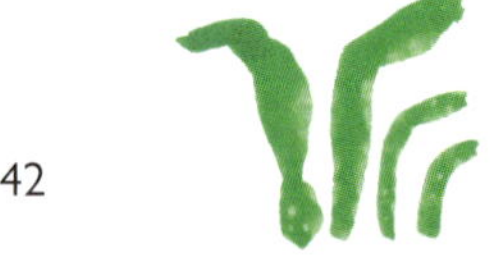

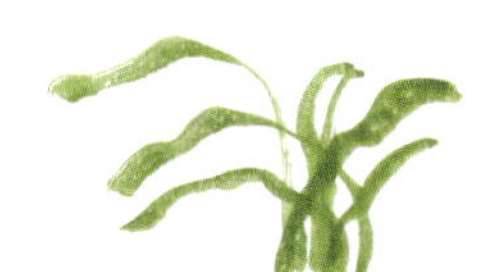

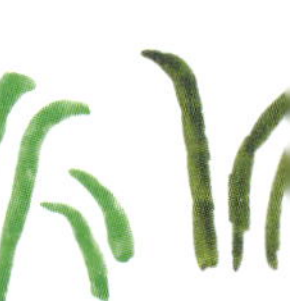

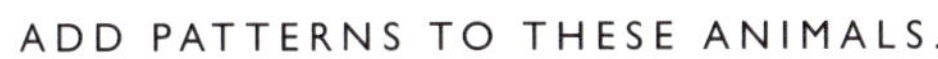

ADD PATTERNS TO THESE ANIMALS.

Mark make, play around with your materials and add your own animals to the blank spaces.

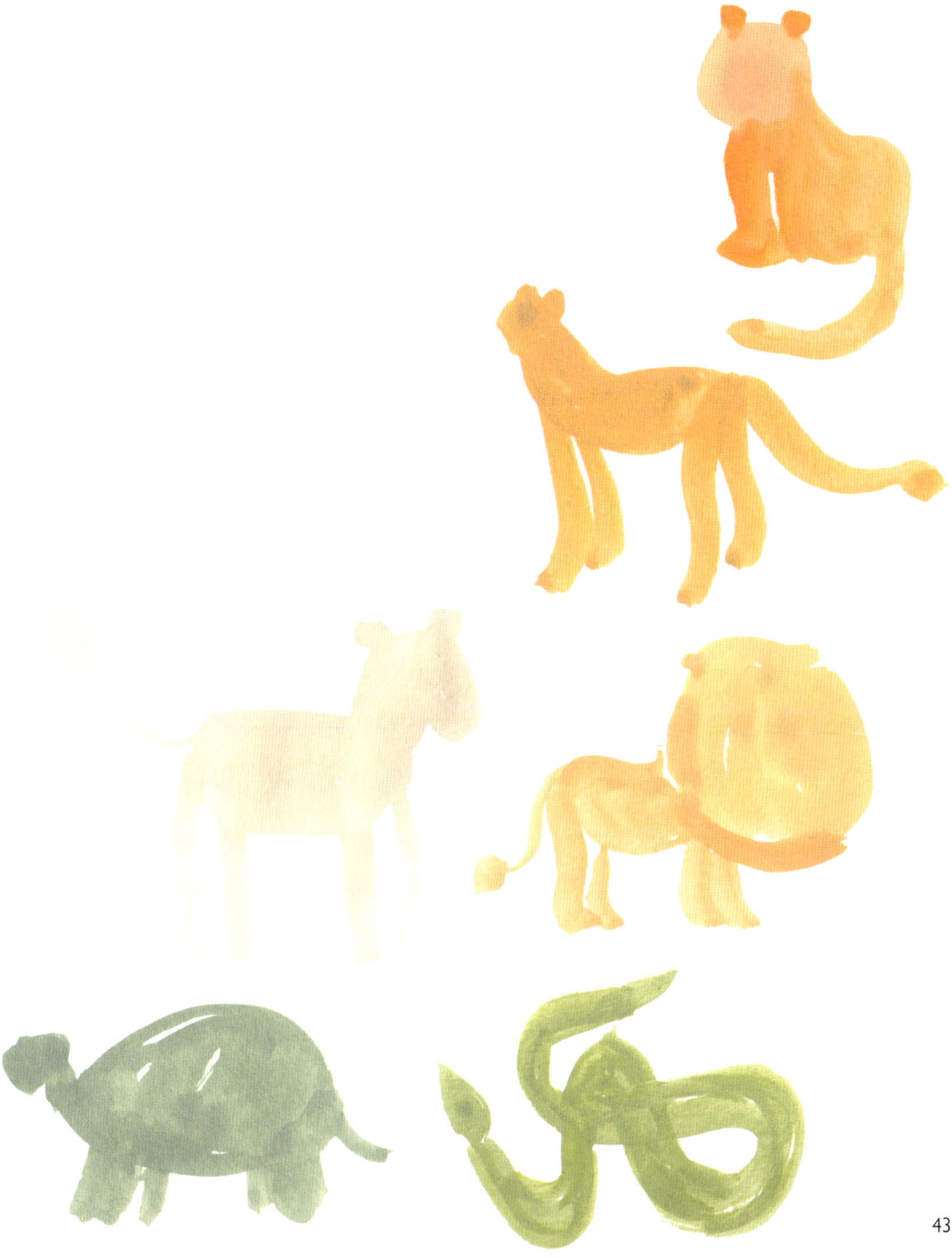

ADD DETAILS TO THE BLANK SPACES TO MAKE THEM INTO ANIMALS.

Use one colour. What animals can you see?

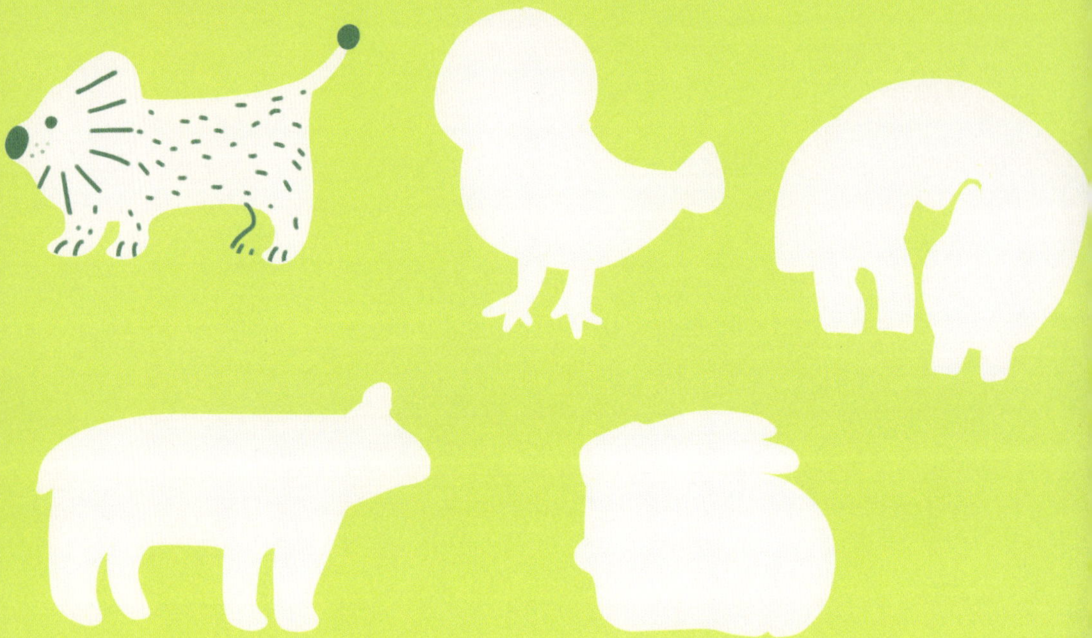

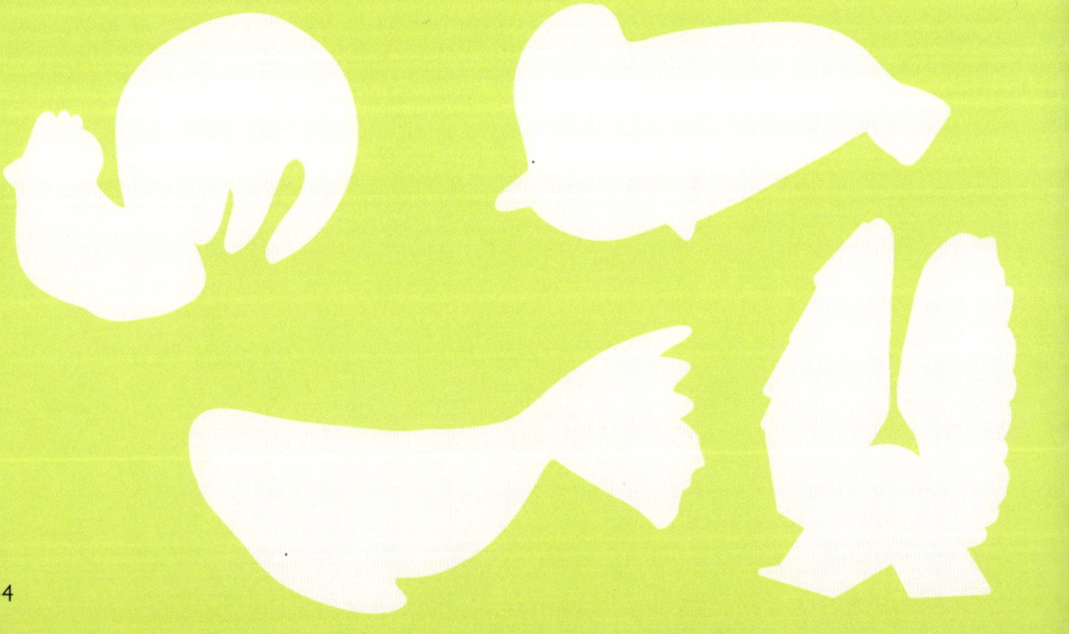

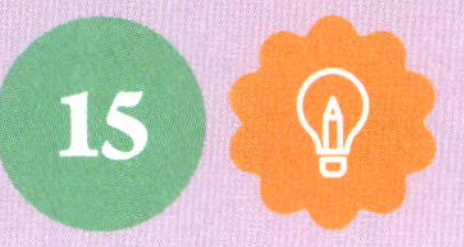

FOLLOWING THE GUIDELINES, DRAW A GARDENER SOWING SEEDS AND NURTURING THEM UNTIL THEY BLOSSOM.

Use any colours and materials you like!

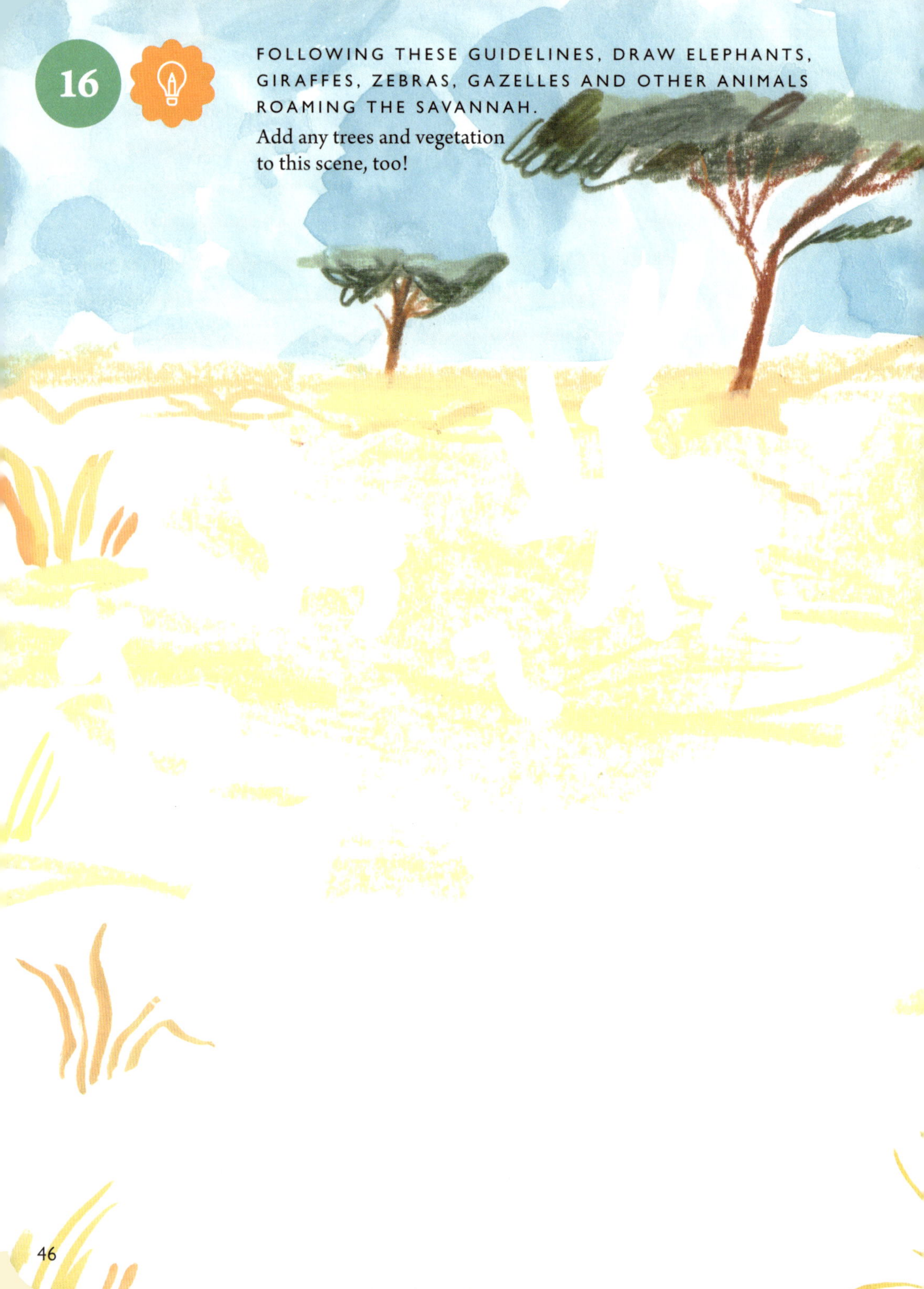

16

FOLLOWING THESE GUIDELINES, DRAW ELEPHANTS, GIRAFFES, ZEBRAS, GAZELLES AND OTHER ANIMALS ROAMING THE SAVANNAH.

Add any trees and vegetation to this scene, too!

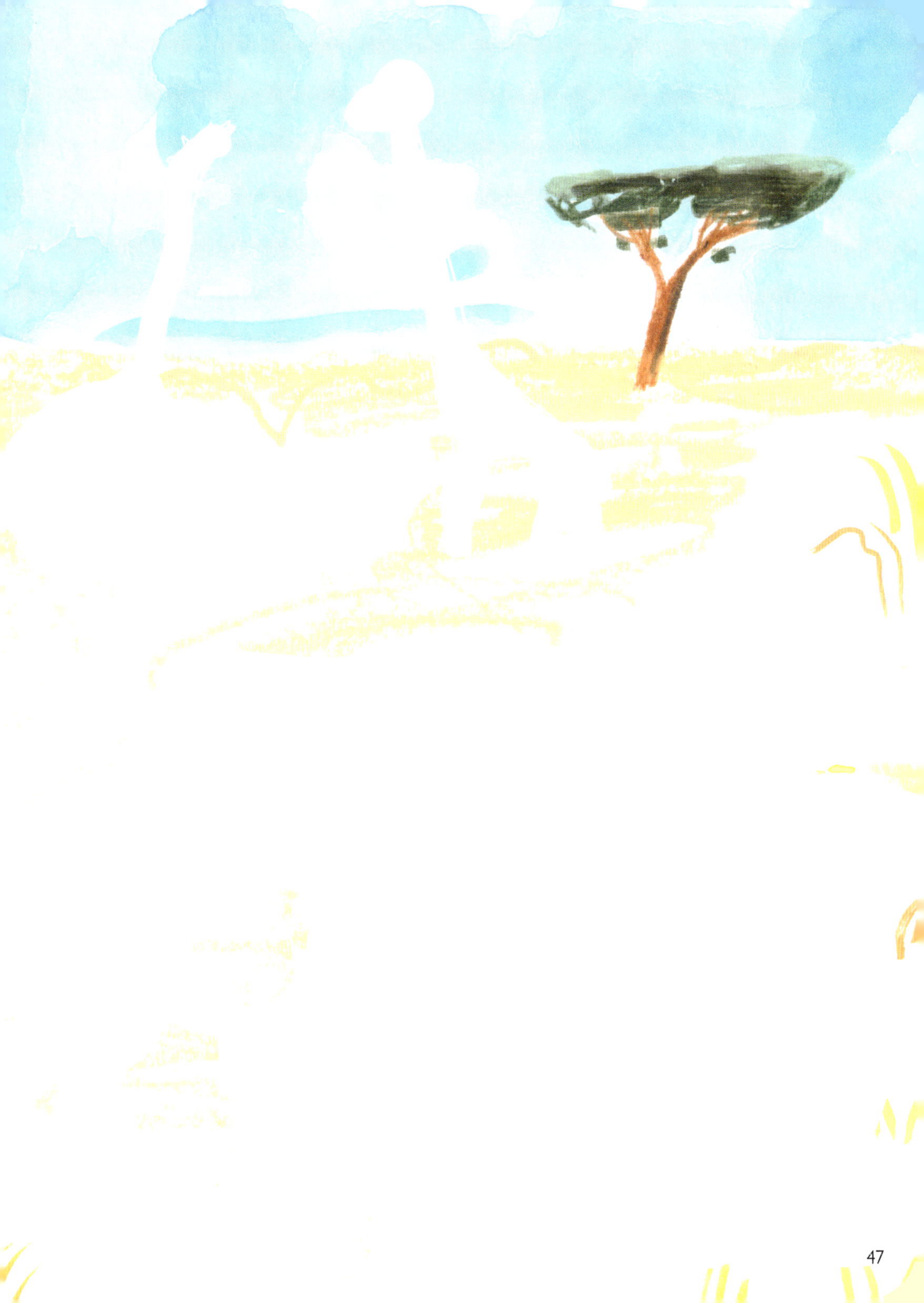

DRAW WHAT YOU CAN SEE IN YOUR LOCAL FOREST OR PARK.

What types of trees are there? Are there any berries or mushrooms? Moss?

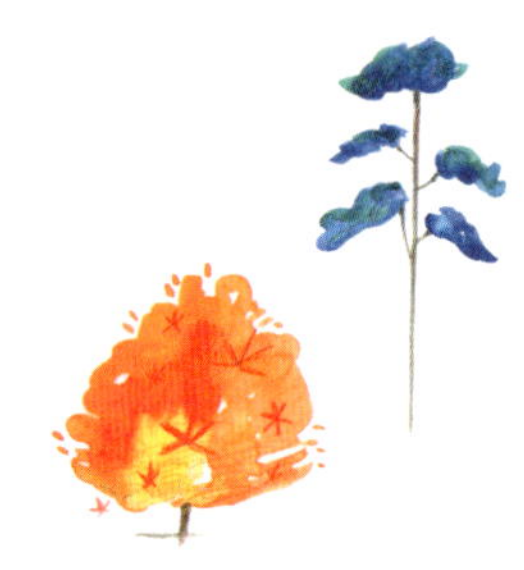

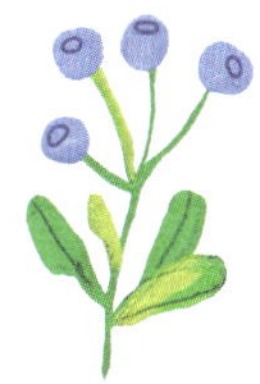

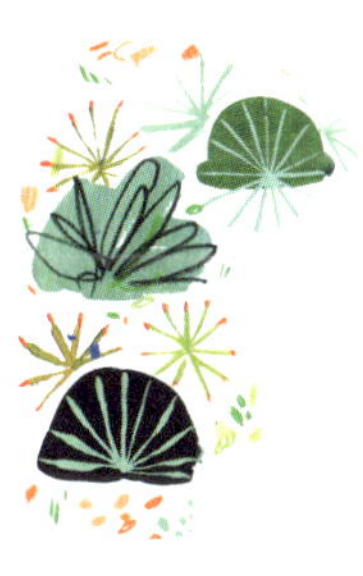

DRAW THE OUTLINES OF INSECTS IN ONE CONTINUOUS LINE WITHOUT TAKING THE PENCIL OFF THE PAPER.

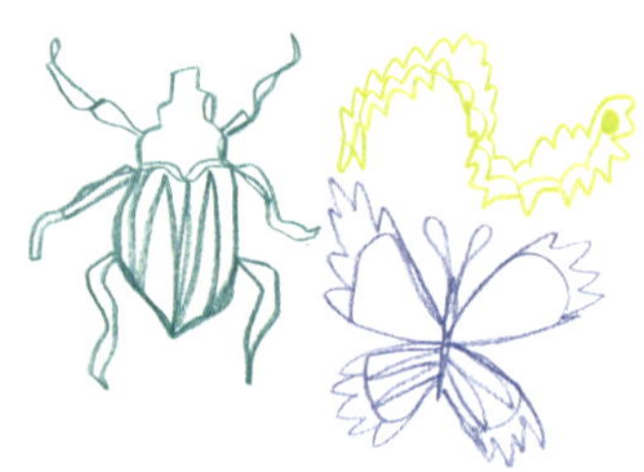

DRAW THE OUTLINES OF FISH, THEN FILL THEM IN COMPLETELY!

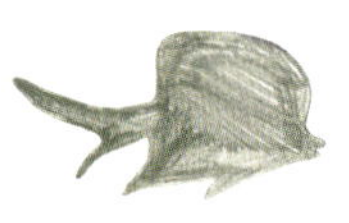

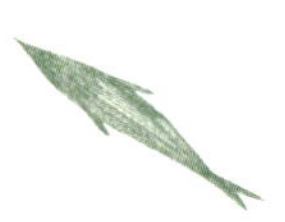

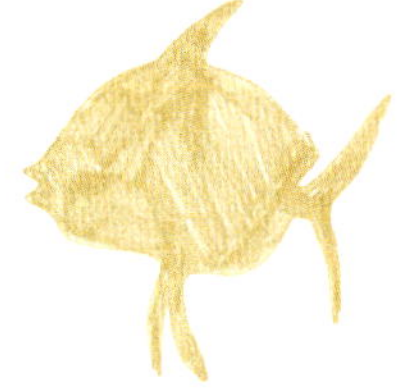

COLLECT COLOUR INSPIRATION FROM INSECTS AND FISH YOU SPOT IN THE WILD TO CREATE YOUR OWN PALETTES.

Play around with your materials, overlap colours and add texture to imitate scales, wings, etc.

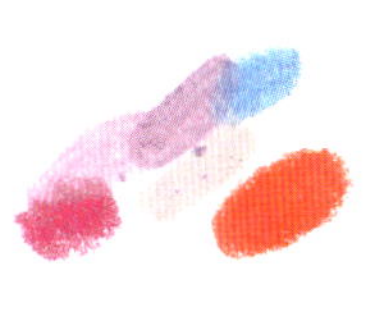
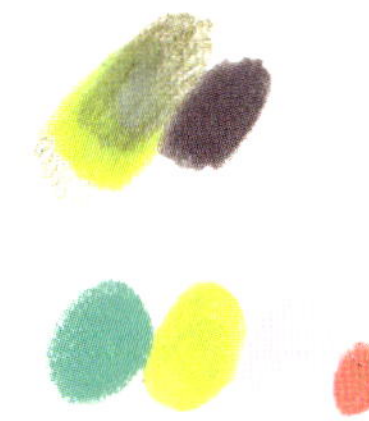

NOW CHOOSE EITHER AN INSECT OR A FISH AND COMBINE IT WITH ONE OF YOUR COLOUR SWATCHES TO CREATE A NEW DRAWING.

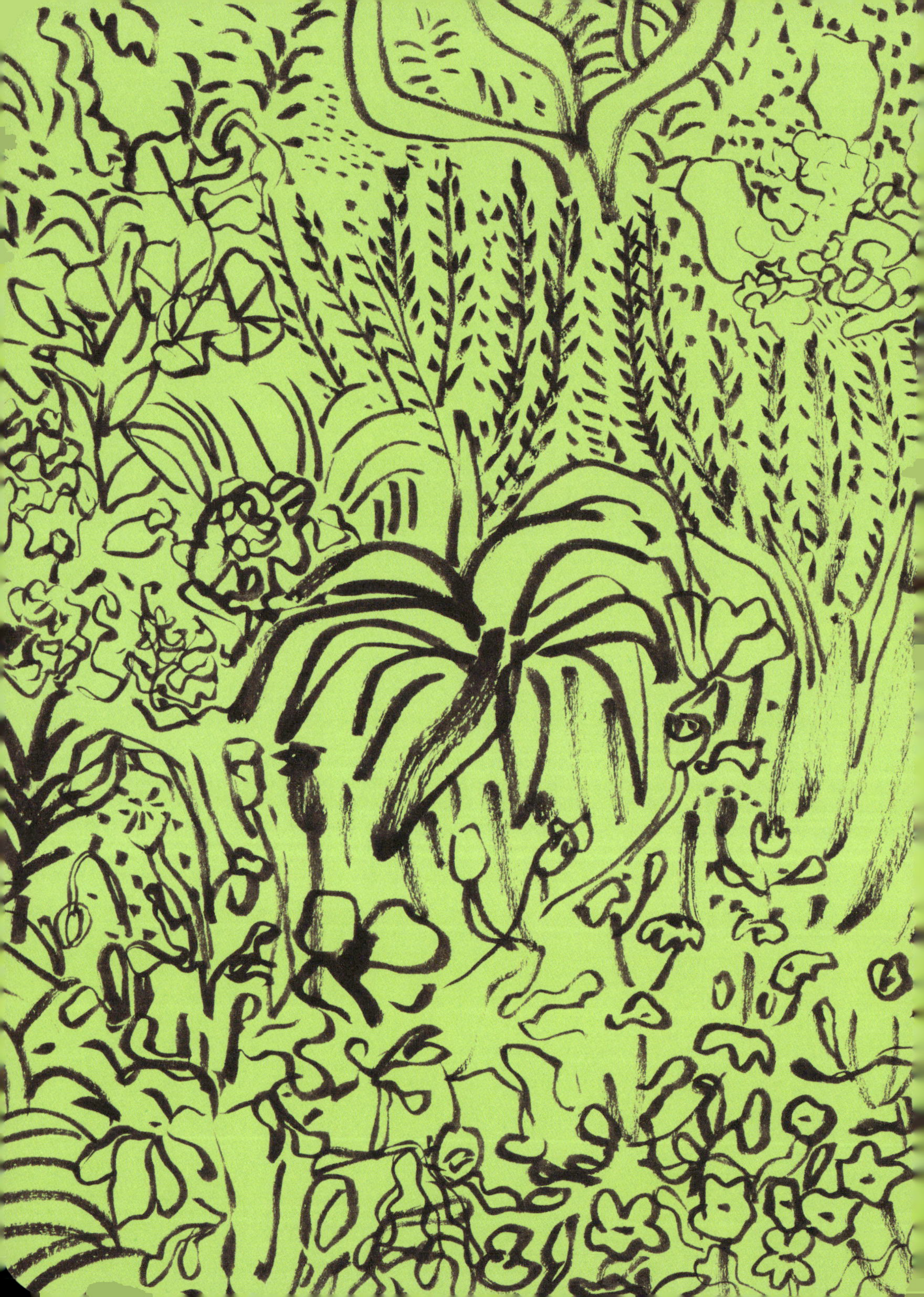

CONTINUE DRAWING THIS GARDEN ON A COLOURED BACKGROUND.

Choose a soft tool, like a brush pen, marker with a flexible nib or a brush with a liquid medium such as ink or watercolour (something like a chunky marker or a crayon will work too). Use expressive strokes to drag, squish and tap your tool and medium, making wide, thin, light and heavy marks. Explore the range of marks you can create, filling in the whole page.

USE THE SHAPES BELOW TO EXPERIMENT WITH THE DIFFERENT FACIAL EXPRESSIONS A CAT MIGHT HAVE.

Changing the position and shape of the ears, and the size and shape of the eyes, for example, will completely change a cat's face. Bigger eyes will appear cuter. Round eyes will appear friendlier, sharper eyes more sceptical.

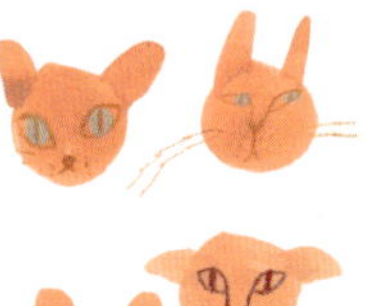

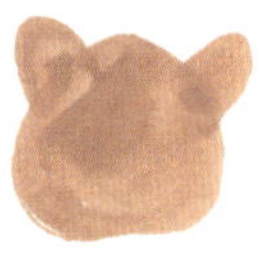
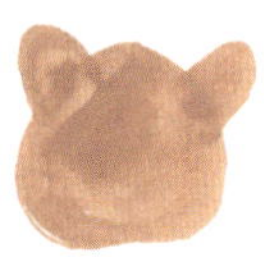
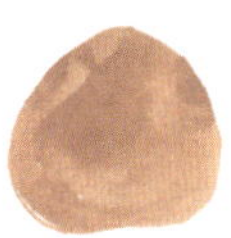
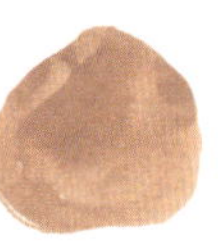
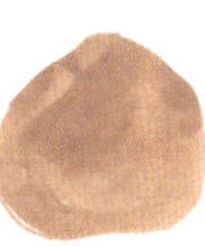
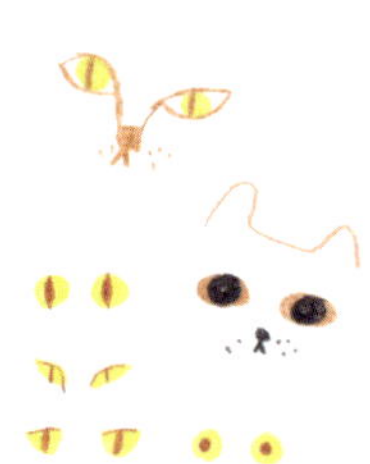

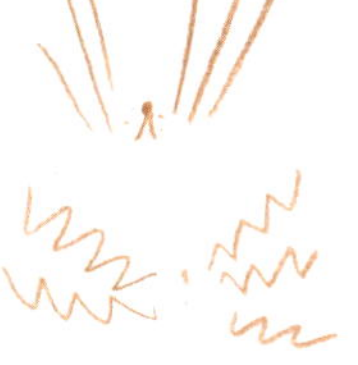

DRAW CATS IN DIFFERENT POSES IN ONE CONTINUOUS LINE WITHOUT TAKING YOUR PENCIL OFF THE PAGE.

This will help you capture the movement of the cats.

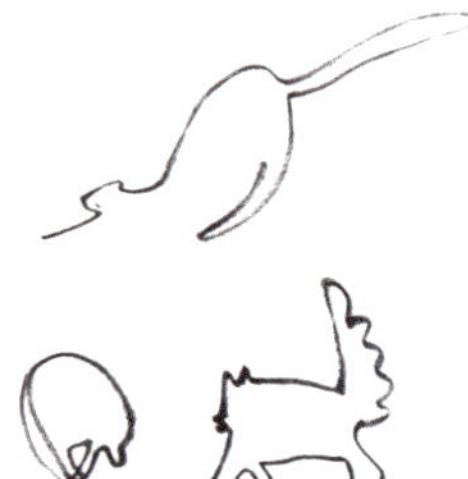

NOW, KEEPING IN MIND THE PREVIOUS TWO EXERCISES, DRAW DIFFERENT CATS WITH VARIOUS EXPRESSIONS AND IN DIFFERENT POSES.

Use full colour this time.

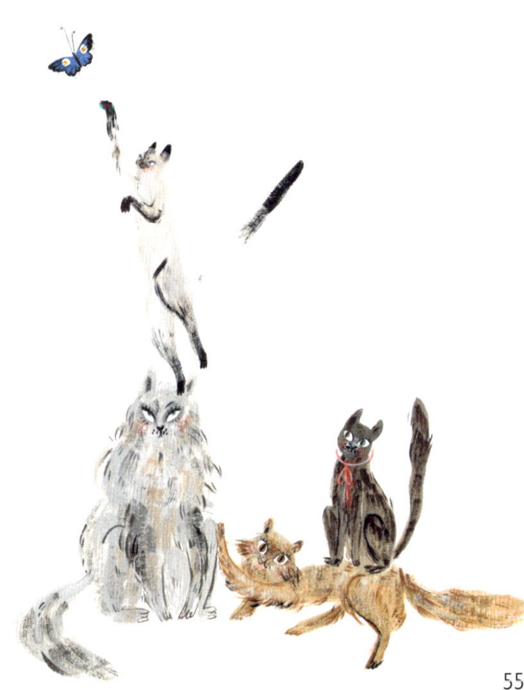

26

PET PORTRAIT STEP-BY-STEP

MATERIALS:
A4 or A5 sheet of paper
Graphite pencil
Eraser
Brush pen, pen, paintbrush or marker

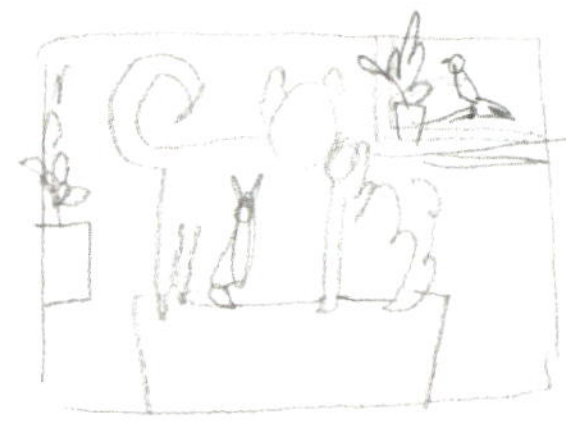

STEP 1

Working with the graphite pencil, create textured lines using the five-step method (see page 6–19) to sketch the composition of a cat with a medium-sized dog next to it and a large dog behind them. Sketch a carpet beneath them and add a window with a view of a bird in the background.

Use geometric shapes for the heads, noses and bodies.

STEP 2

Once you are happy with the composition, simplify the abstract shapes, erase the guidelines and add a few more details. Think about different textures and faces for the animals. And feel free to add plant pots, patterns on the carpet and pictures on the walls.

STEP 3

Using a brush pen or other tool of your choice, fill in the cat all black apart from the eyes. Use the same tool to add facial features to the dogs, including the eyes, nose and whiskers, and the bird.

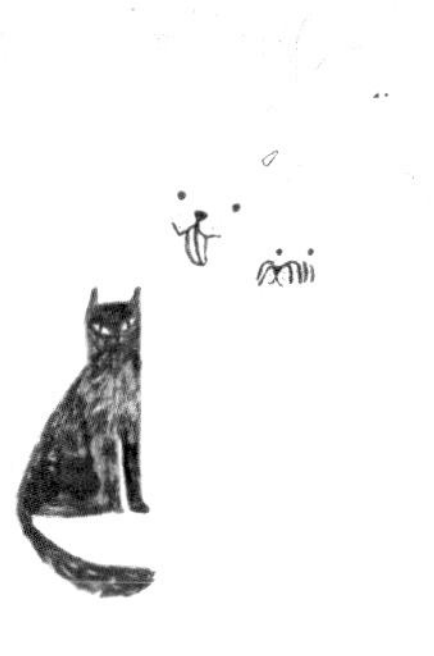

STEP 4

Use the same tool to enhance the branches the bird is perched on, the bird's body and other details in your scene.

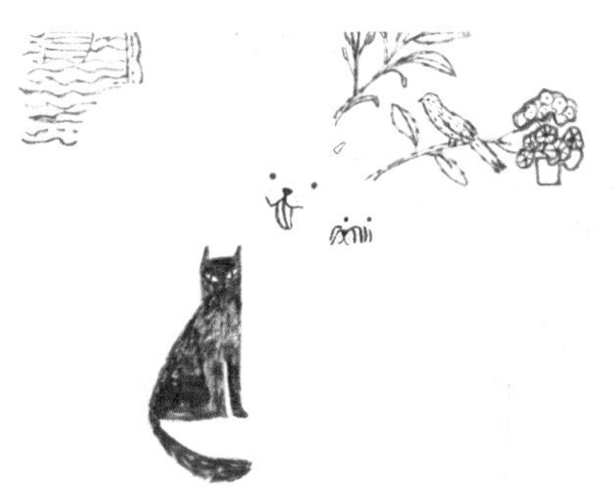

STEP 5

Keep adding patterns and details to the elements of your drawing.

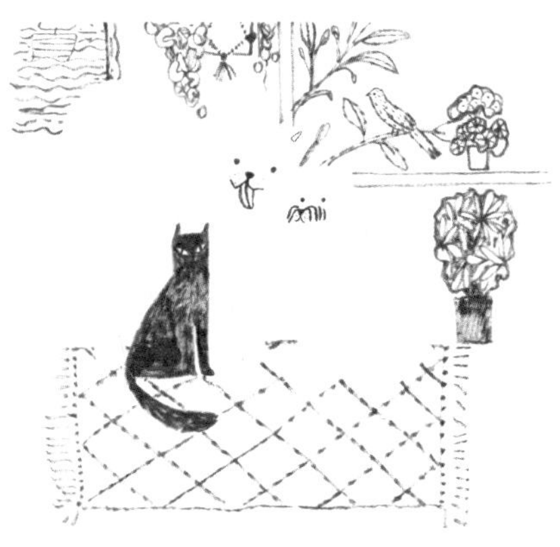

STEP 6

Now add texture to the dogs, creating different patterns for their fur.

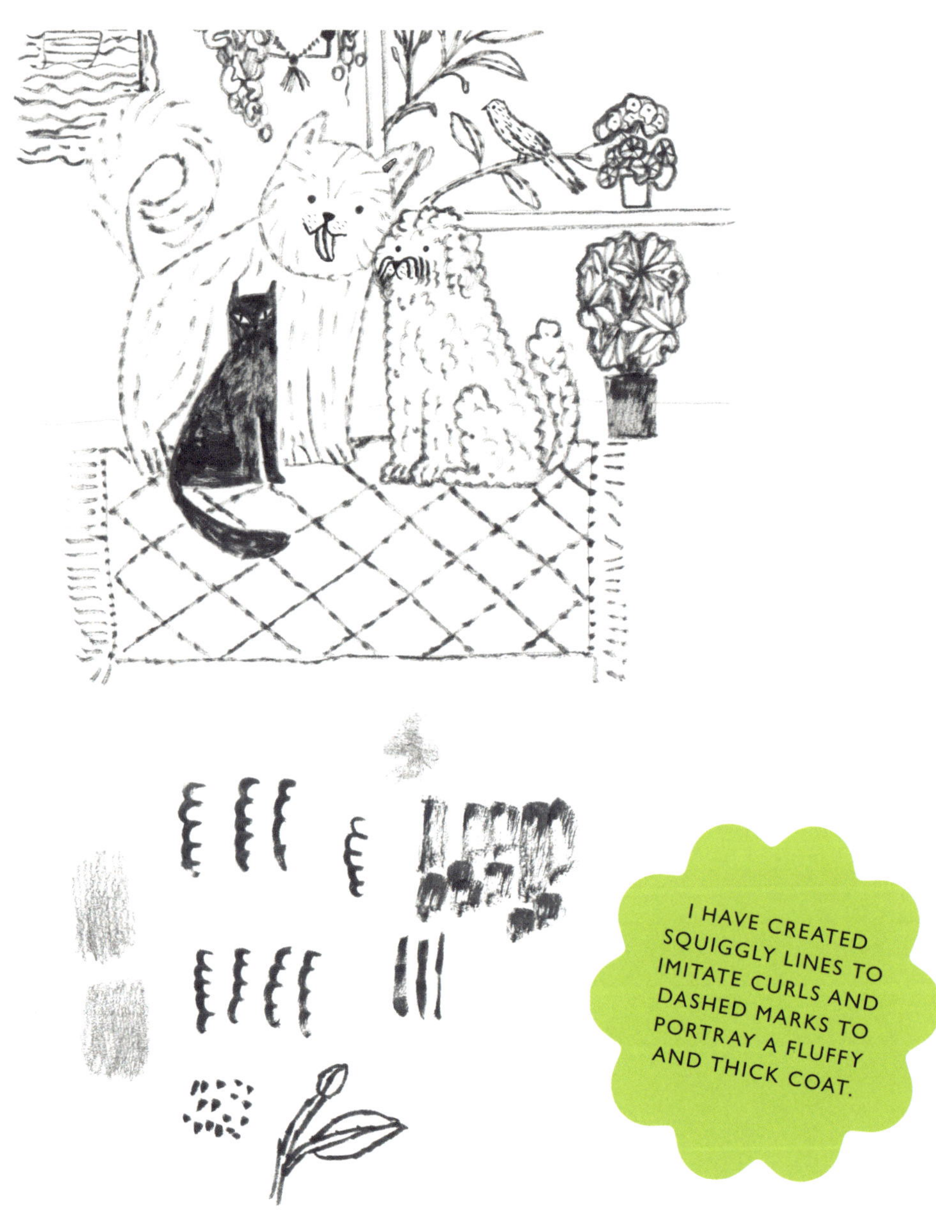

I HAVE CREATED SQUIGGLY LINES TO IMITATE CURLS AND DASHED MARKS TO PORTRAY A FLUFFY AND THICK COAT.

STEP 7

Add whiskers to the cat and, if you have white paint, draw on a little nose and paw details. Fill in the background with graphite pencil in a light grey and add more branches outside the window.

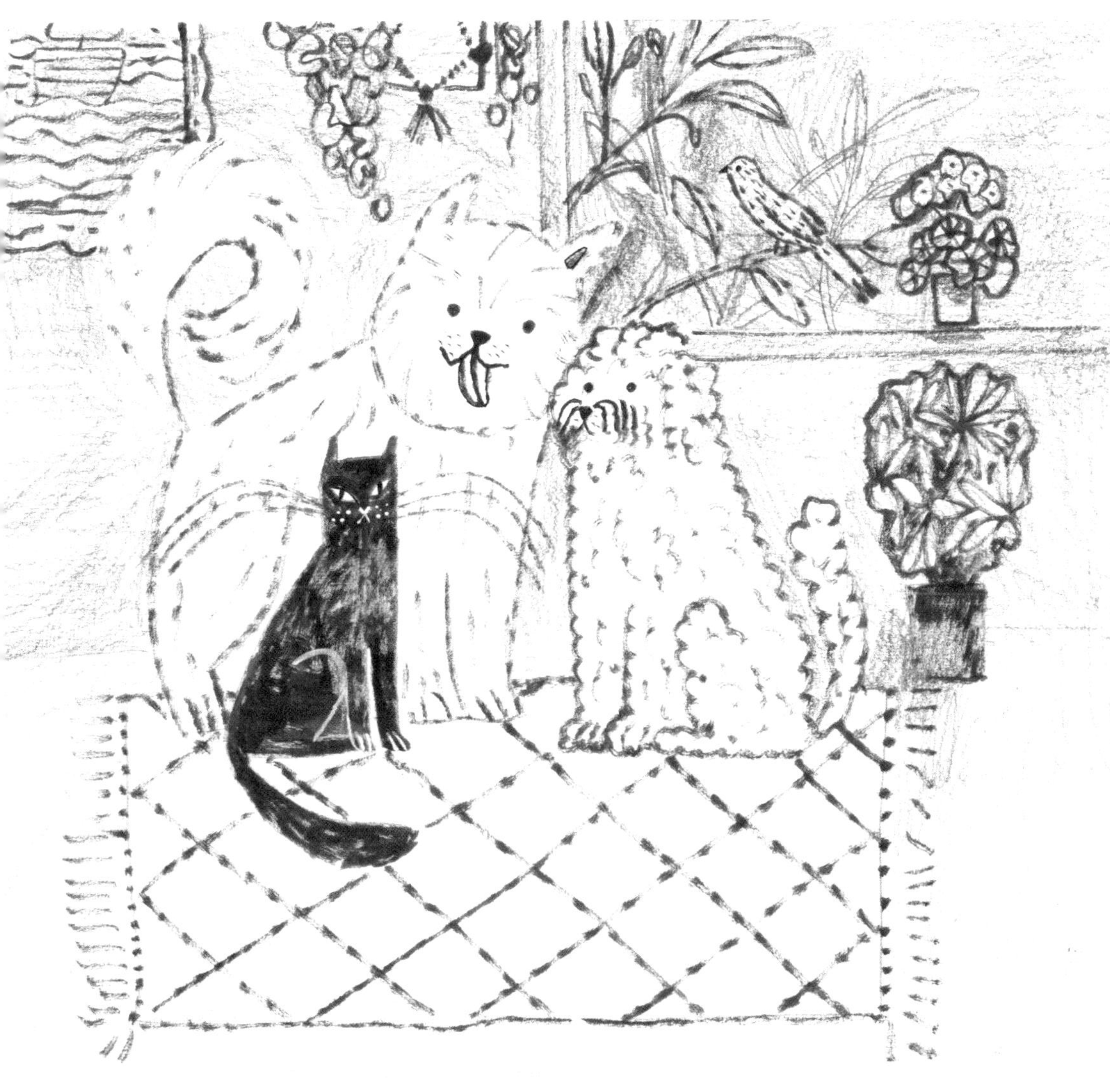

DRAW THE SEA AND THE BEACH FOR THESE PEOPLE.

Play around with your tools, mark make and think about the rhythms of the water and the beach (is it sand, rocks or sandy grass, for example?)

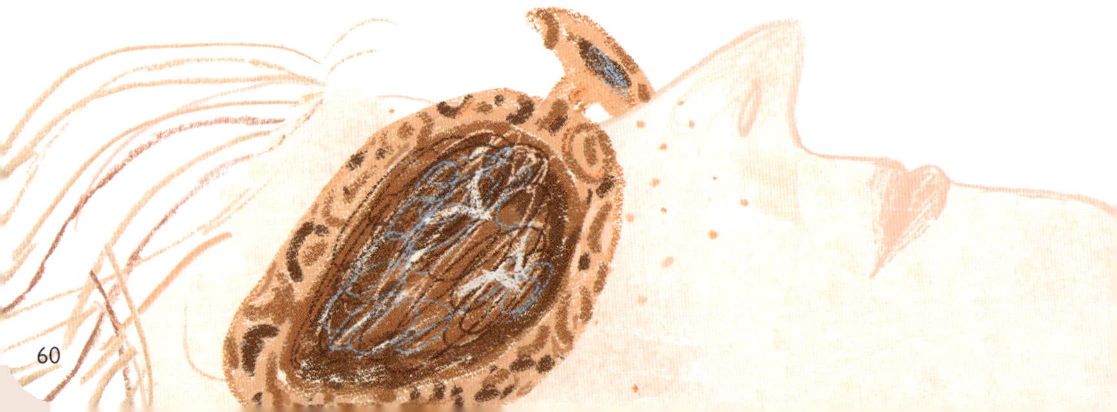

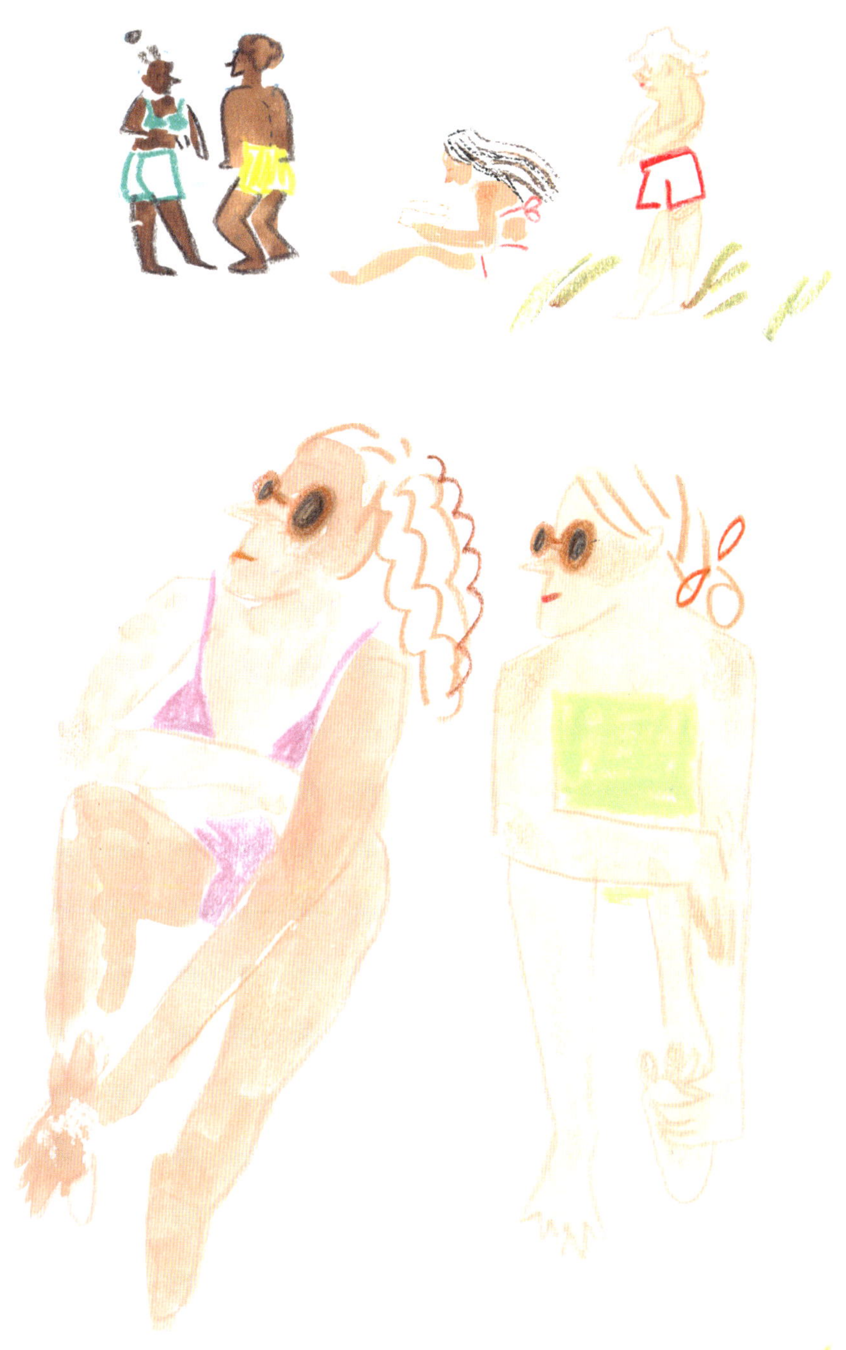

NATURE CREATES AN ENDLESS VARIETY
OF SHAPES, FORMS, SIZES AND TEXTURES.

Let's look closer at shell shapes. The shell is a house, a skeleton and sometimes even a vehicle. Fill in this page with shells in different sizes and shapes, and draw them from a variety of angles. Think about lines and mark making and use one colour.

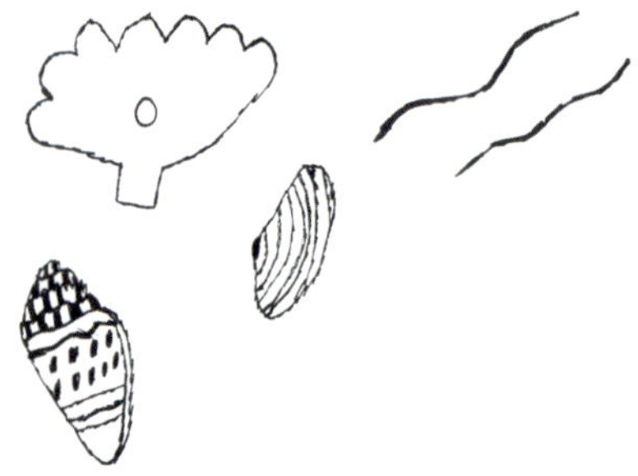

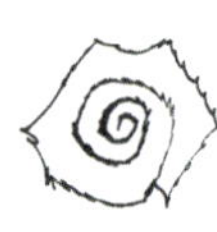

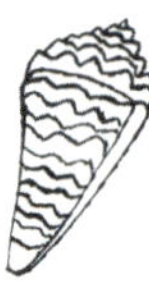

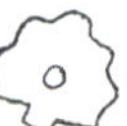

USE YOUR FAVOURITE SHELLS FROM THE PREVIOUS PLAY AND USE THEM TO CREATE A SEA-THEMED DRAWING.

Add other ocean-themed elements, such as seaweed and fish, to create a pretty composition.

IN THE ARTWORKS ON THE LEFT-HAND SIDE, I HAVE USED OVALS TO CREATE THE HEADS AND BODIES OF THE BIRDS.

This helps to create a more realistic style of drawing. My other style is to draw bold outlines, usually without taking the pencil off the paper to exaggerate certain features (see illustrations on the right). This often results in more dynamic drawings. Draw a variety of birds, using both methods, and see which one you prefer.

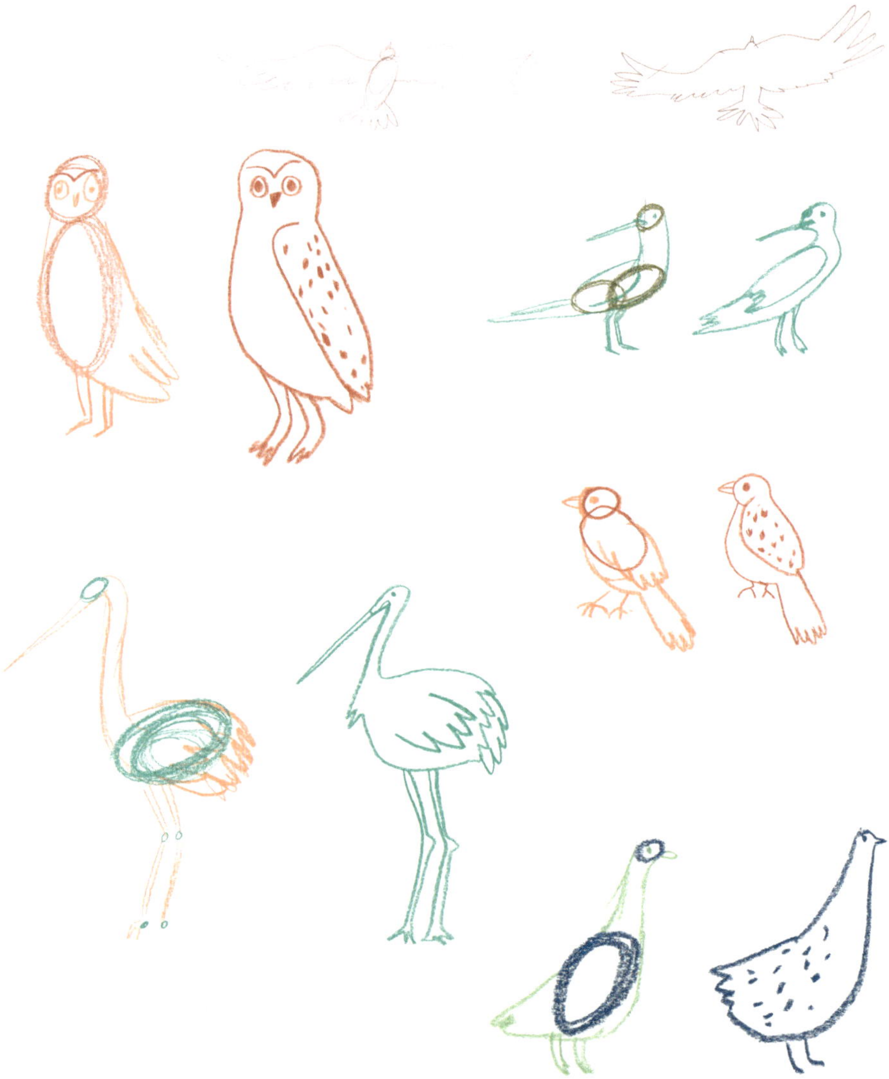

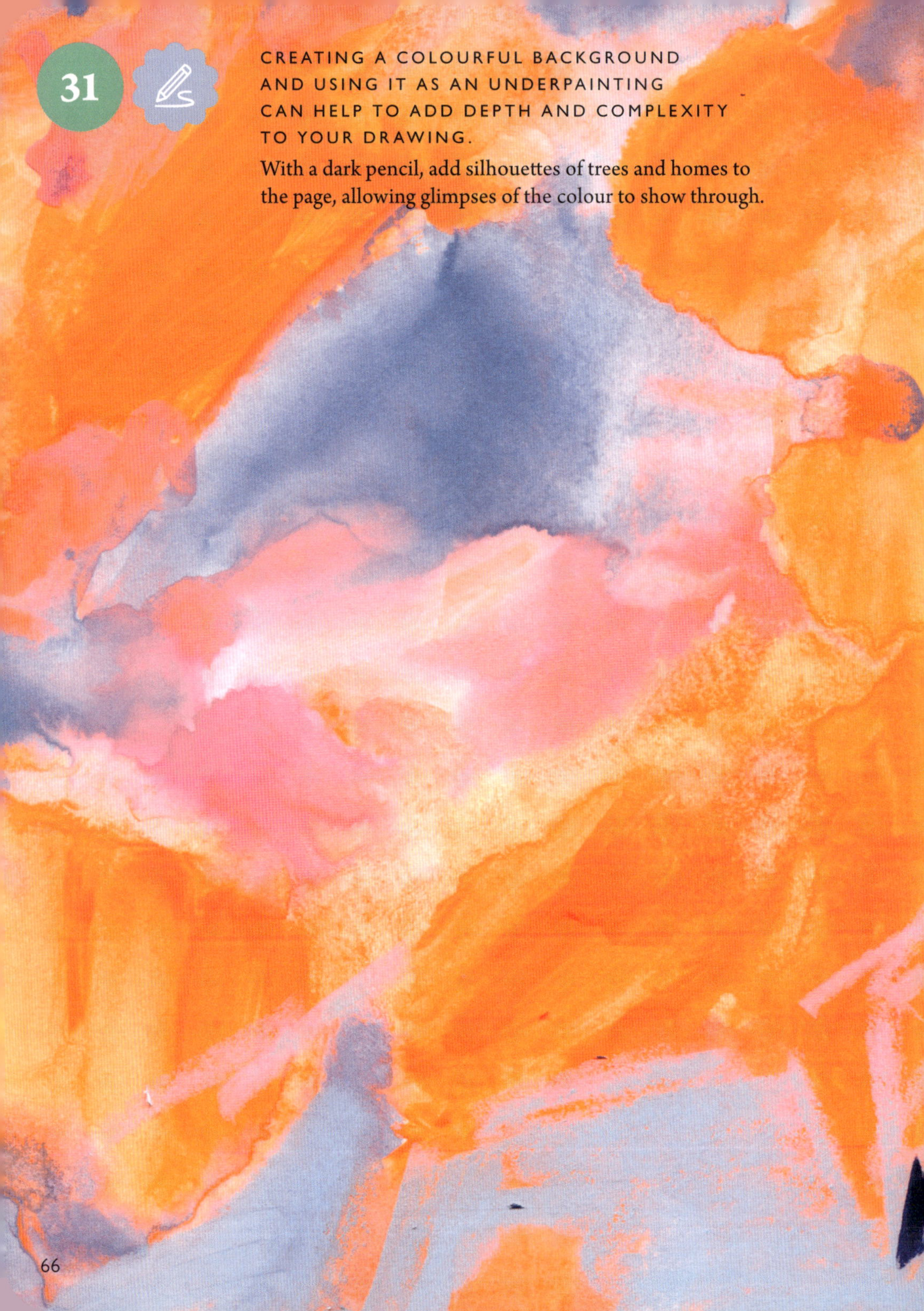

31

CREATING A COLOURFUL BACKGROUND AND USING IT AS AN UNDERPAINTING CAN HELP TO ADD DEPTH AND COMPLEXITY TO YOUR DRAWING.

With a dark pencil, add silhouettes of trees and homes to the page, allowing glimpses of the colour to show through.

CREATE YOUR OWN SUNSET COLOUR UNDERPAINTING. GO WILD WITH COLOURS AND ADD YOUR OWN MATCHING SILHOUETTES.

Draw a sunset scene from where you live now.

33

DRAW ANIMALS, BIRDS, FROGS, ETC. IN THIS JUNGLE SCENE.

Feel free to overlap animals and add more wildlife!

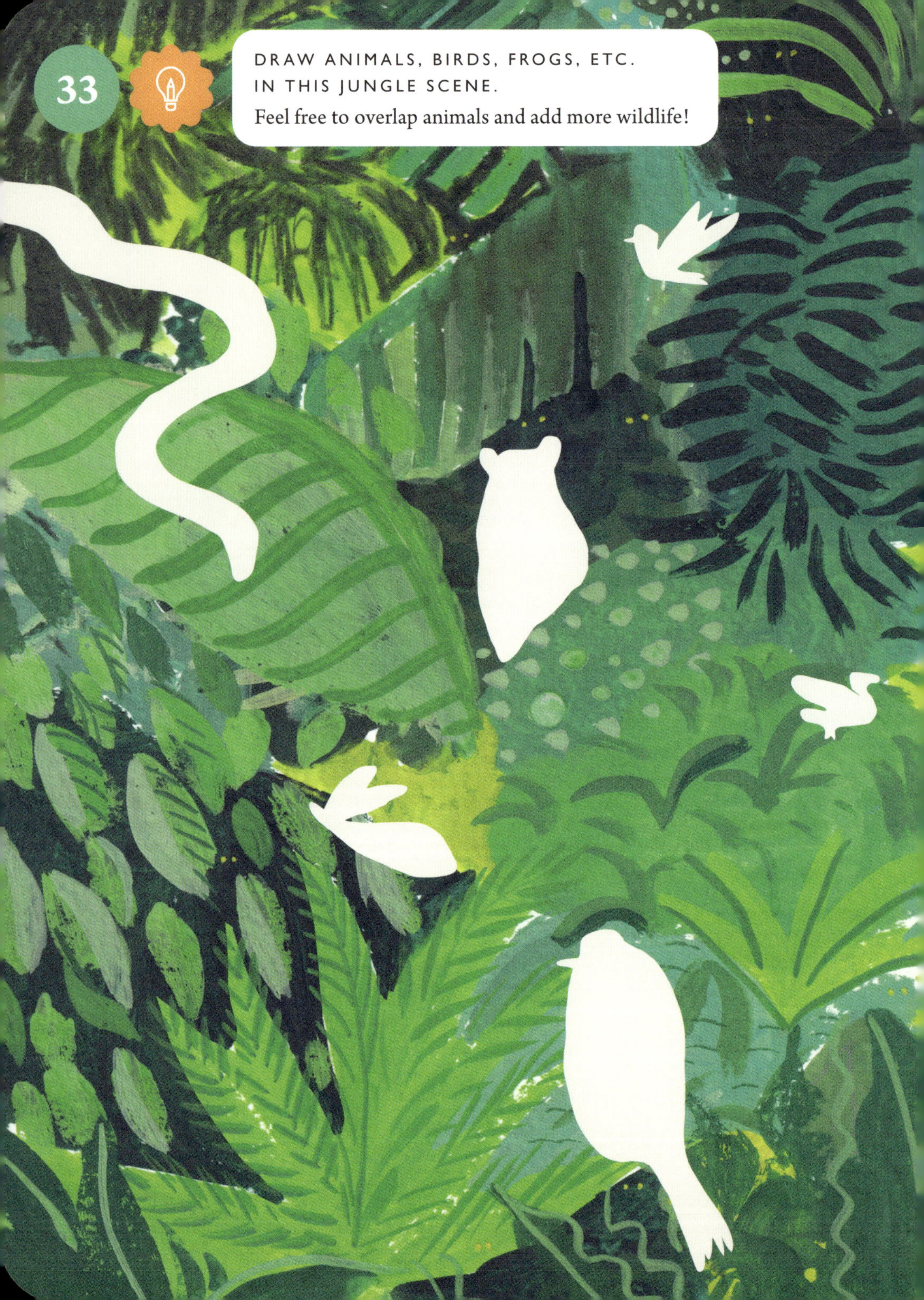

34

CREATE YOUR OWN JUNGLE OR FOREST SCENE, USING THIS PAGE AS AN UNDERPAINTING, AND OVERLAY LEAVES, FOLIAGE, FLOWERS, ETC.

Play around with different tools and materials!

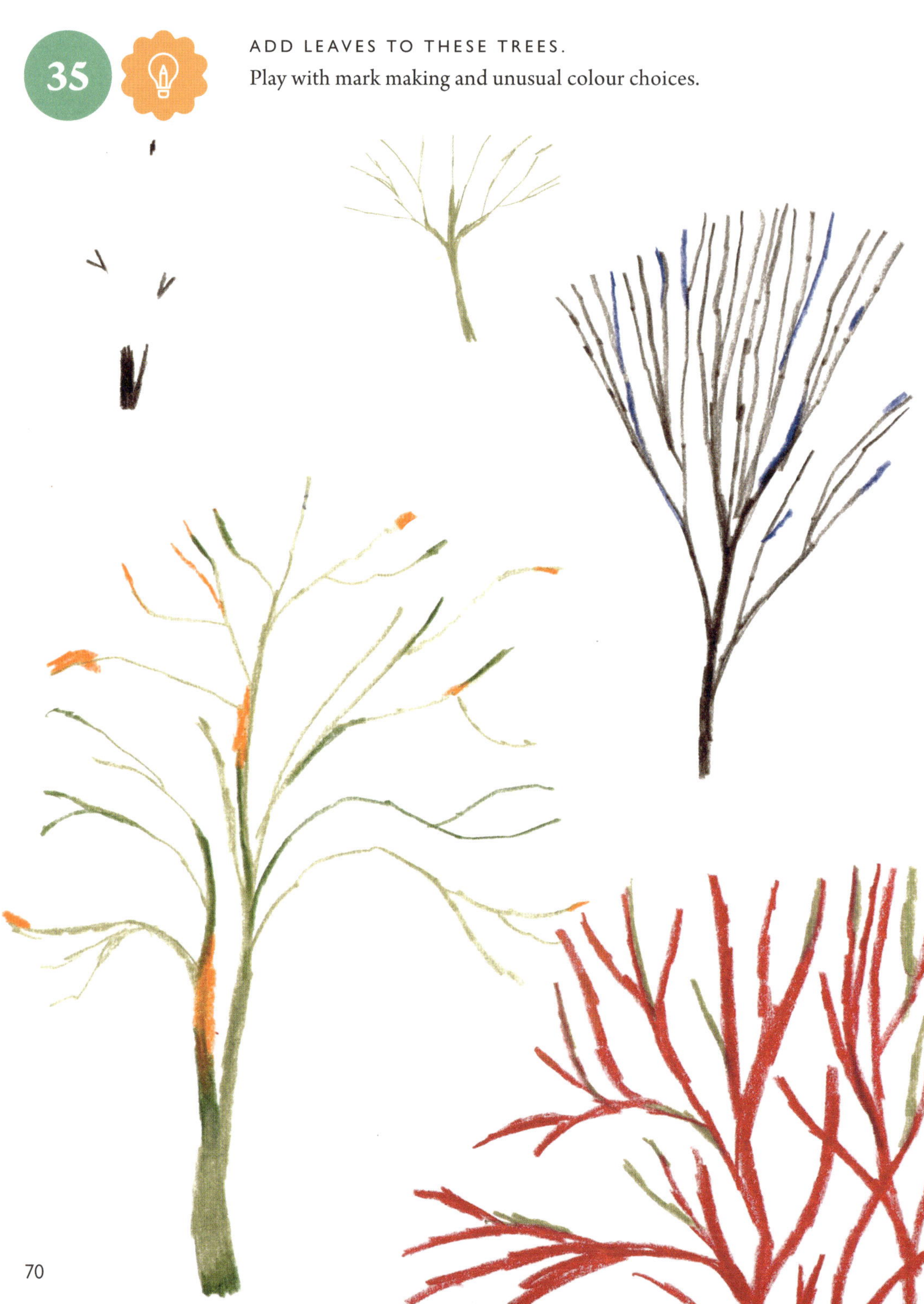
35
ADD LEAVES TO THESE TREES.
Play with mark making and unusual colour choices.

CREATE AN ATMOSPHERIC AND TONALLY DARK DRAWING WITH ONE LIGHT SOURCE.

For example, a cityscape at night with only a handful of windows lit up or a moon above a dark forest.

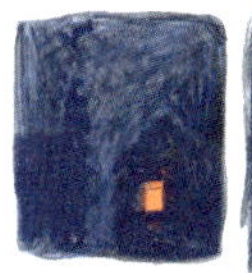

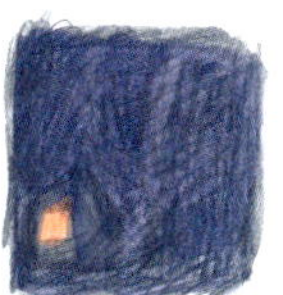

DOGS COME IN SO MANY SHAPES, SIZES AND BREEDS.

Fill in this page with a variety of different dogs.

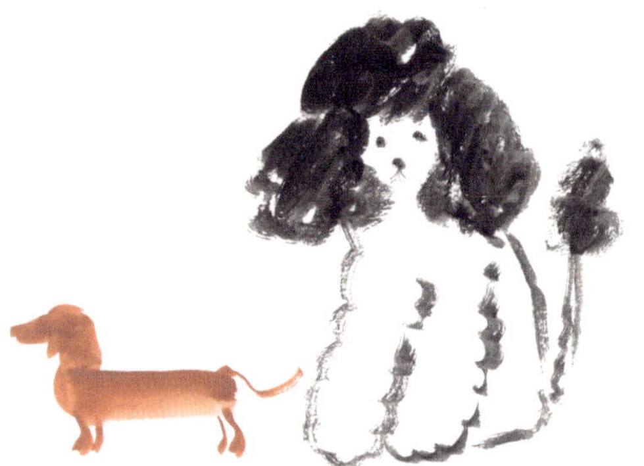

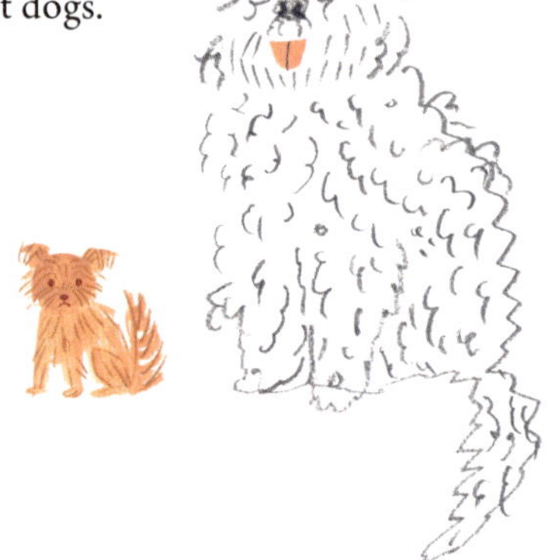

THE SKY IS BLUE AND THE GRASS IS GREEN, RIGHT?

We often let our brains override what we see, but if we look closely we will see a variety of colours. Look at the examples I have drawn and pay attention to the different colours used.

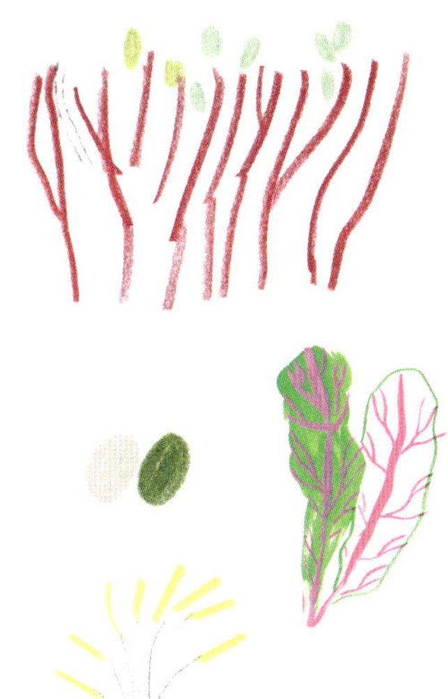

The branch is not just brown but burgundy, with soft pistachio-coloured leaves. Notice what colours are around you, make note of them, and make this page into a collection of surprising colours from your everyday life. Sketch objects and create colour swatches.

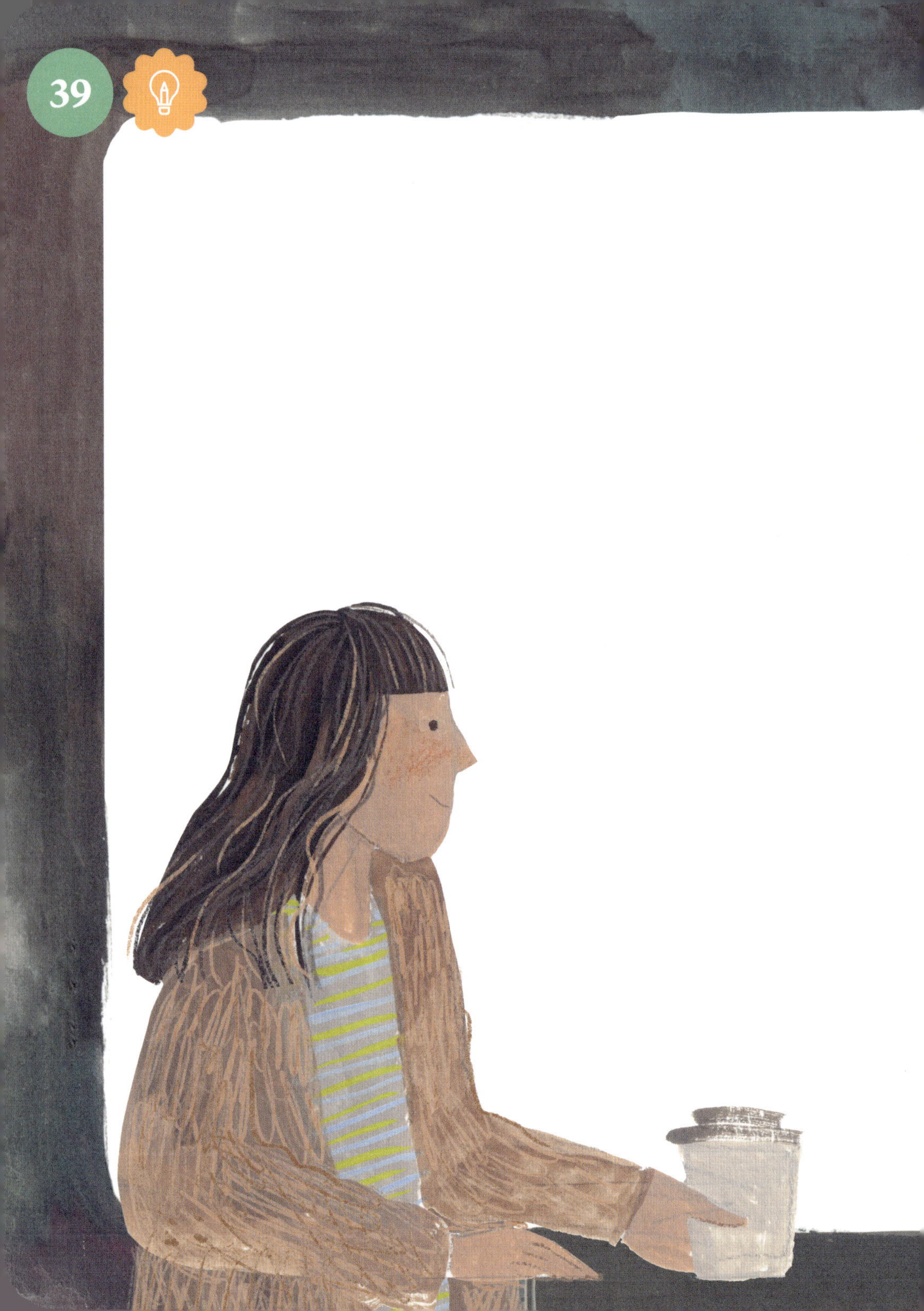
39

DRAW A QUAINT LANDSCAPE FOR THESE TRAIN TRAVELLERS USING THE GUIDELINES.

What season is it? What can they see? Horses, people, sheep, houses?

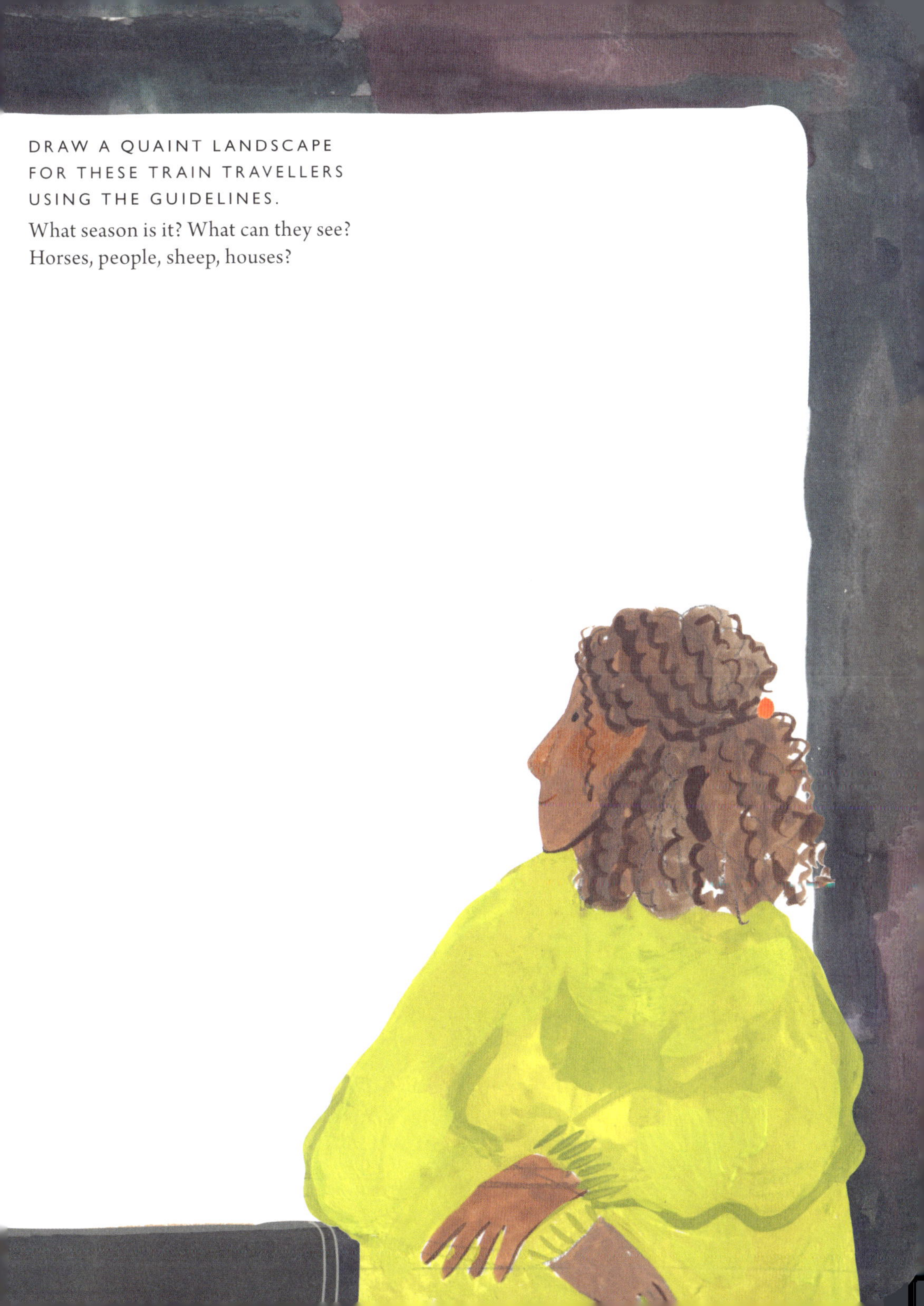

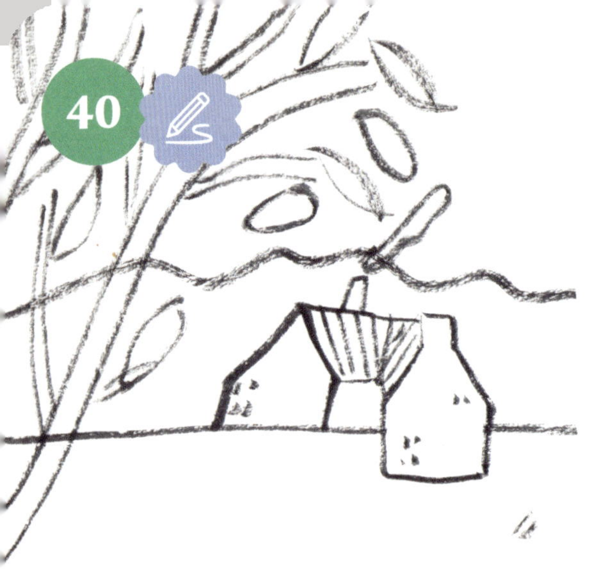

CREATE A SERIES OF DRAWINGS BASED ON THE SAME MOTIF (MAYBE THE VIEW FROM YOUR WINDOW, A FIELD OR HOUSEPLANT) BUT EACH WITH A DIFFERENT FOCUS.

LINE

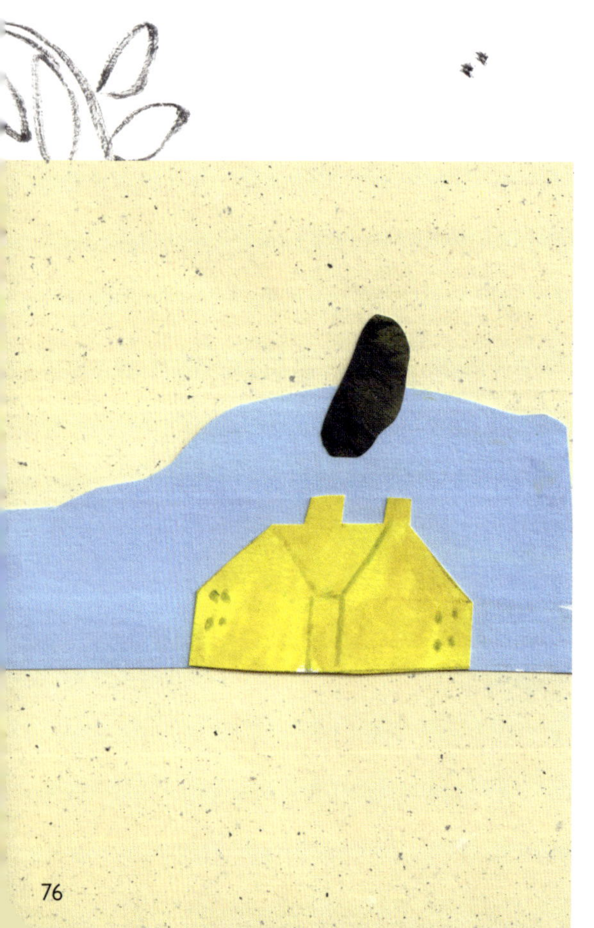

SHAPE

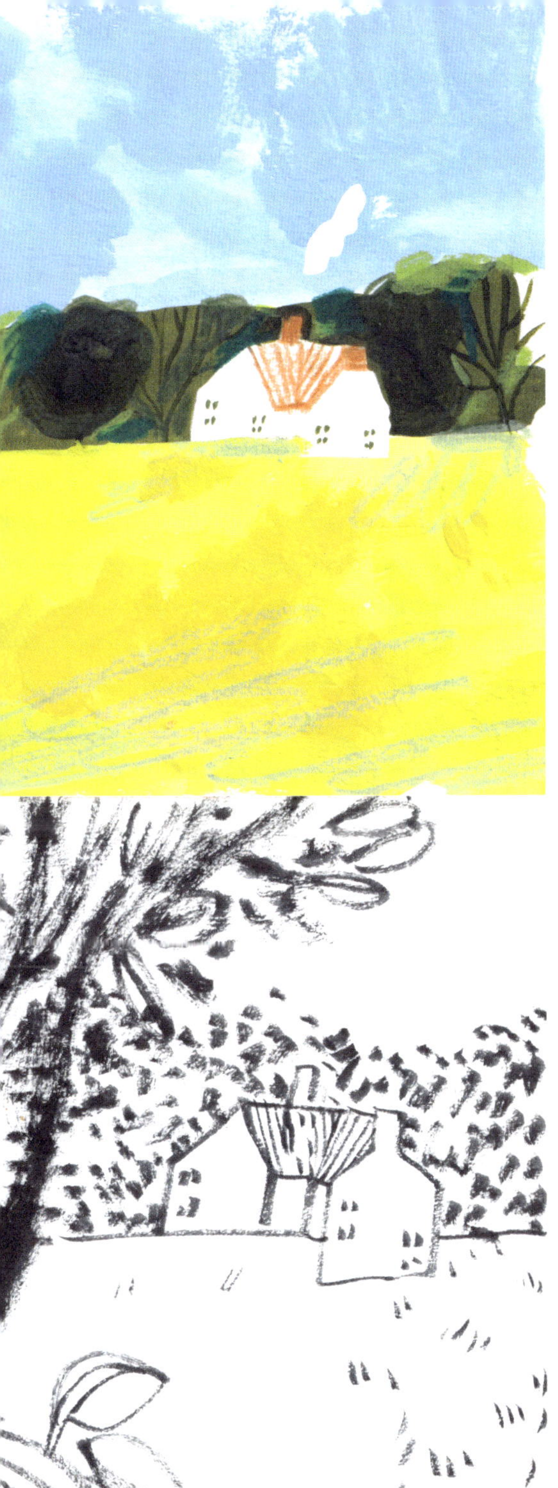

COLOUR

MARK
MAKING

IN ART, NEGATIVE SPACE IS THE SPACE AROUND AND BETWEEN YOUR MAIN SUBJECT.

Let's create a bouquet of flowers using negative space, by drawing the elements around it.

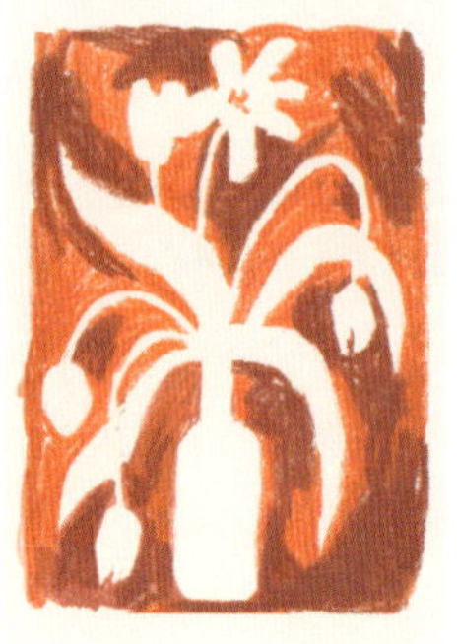

DRAW A PET!

If you don't have a pet, draw
a childhood or imaginary pet.

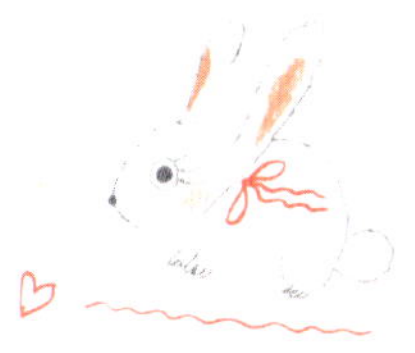

DRAW A COLLECTION OF BERRIES, LEAVES AND FLOWERS IN THE SQUARES USING ONE COLOUR ONLY.

Think about lines, shapes and negative space.

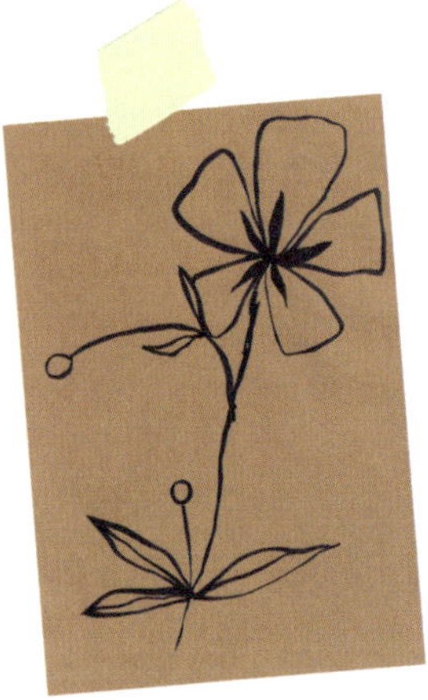

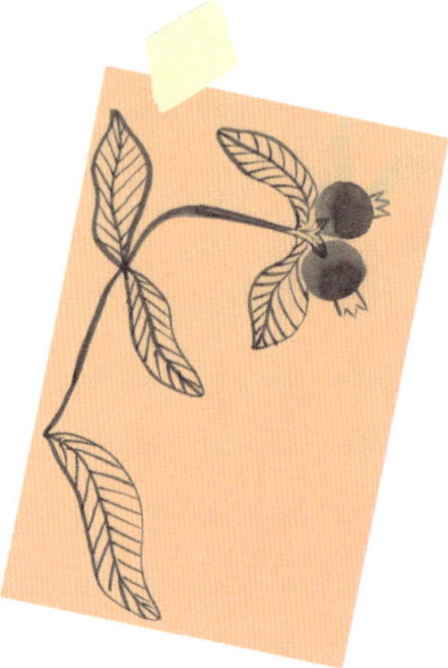

DRAW A PARK SCENE, ADDING TREES, GRASS AND HOUSES.

Feel free to follow the guidelines or add your own pieces of nature. Frame the scene by adding bushes and branches in the foreground – this is a really fun way to create an interesting composition.

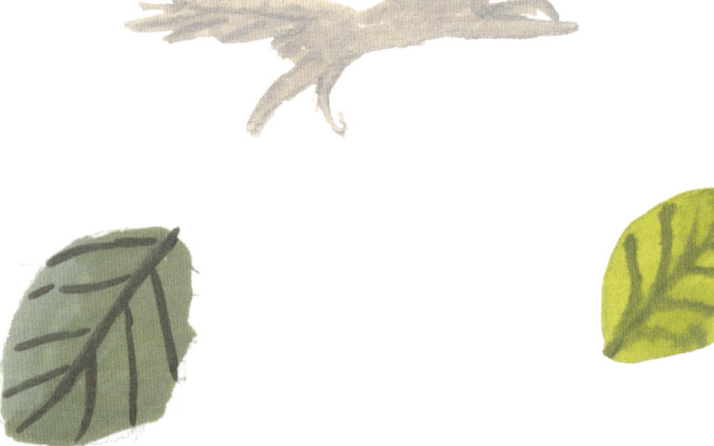

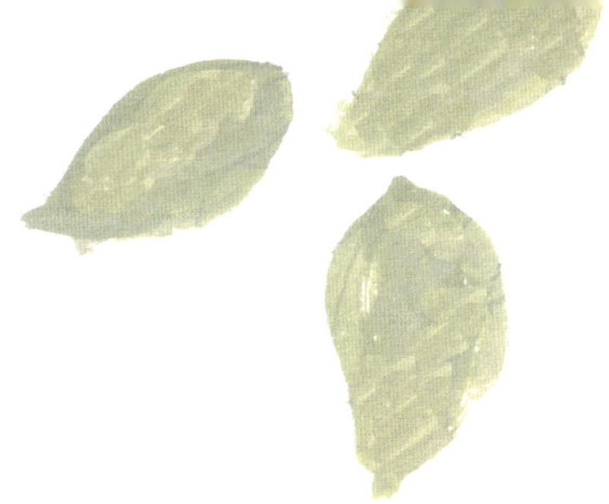

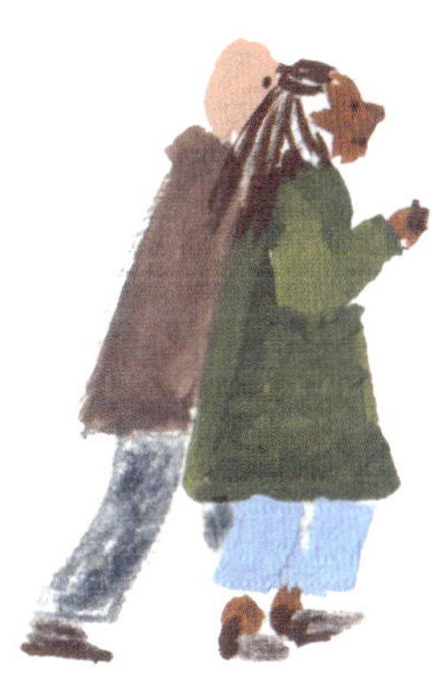

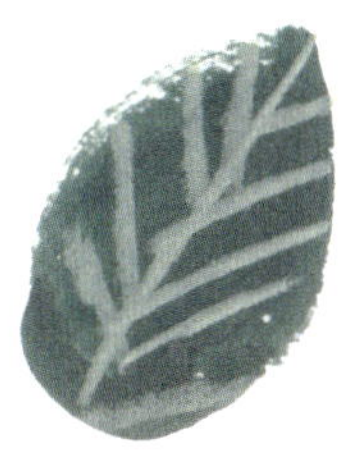

PETS OFTEN LOOK LIKE THEIR OWNERS.

Draw matching pets for these people.

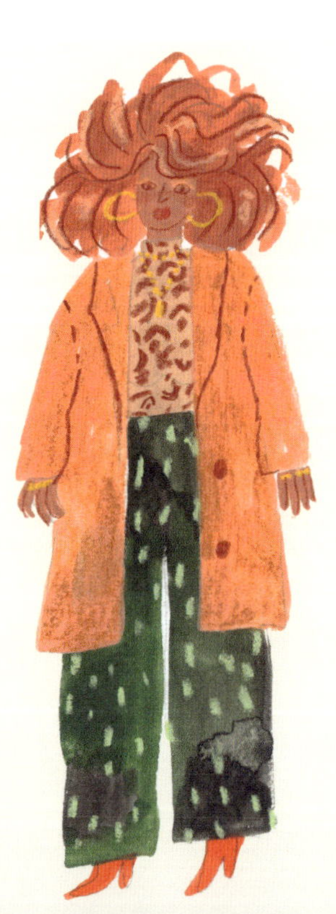

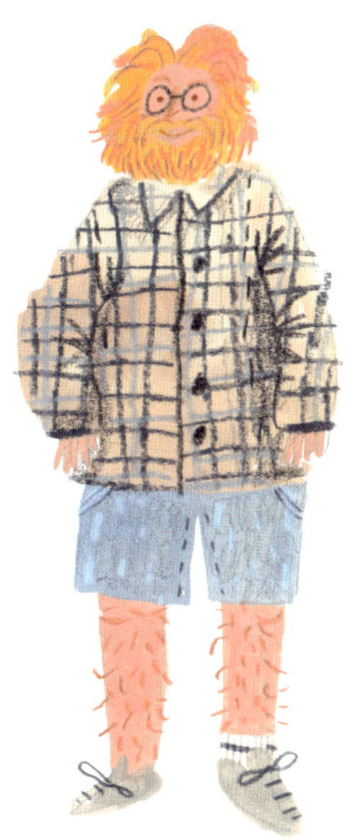

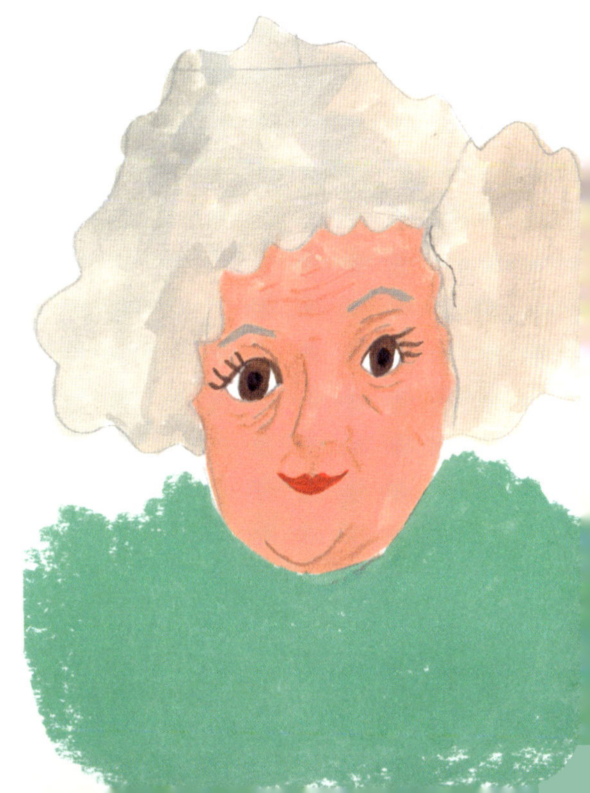

DRAW A PARK FOR THESE PEOPLE.

Add your own trees, grass and flowers.

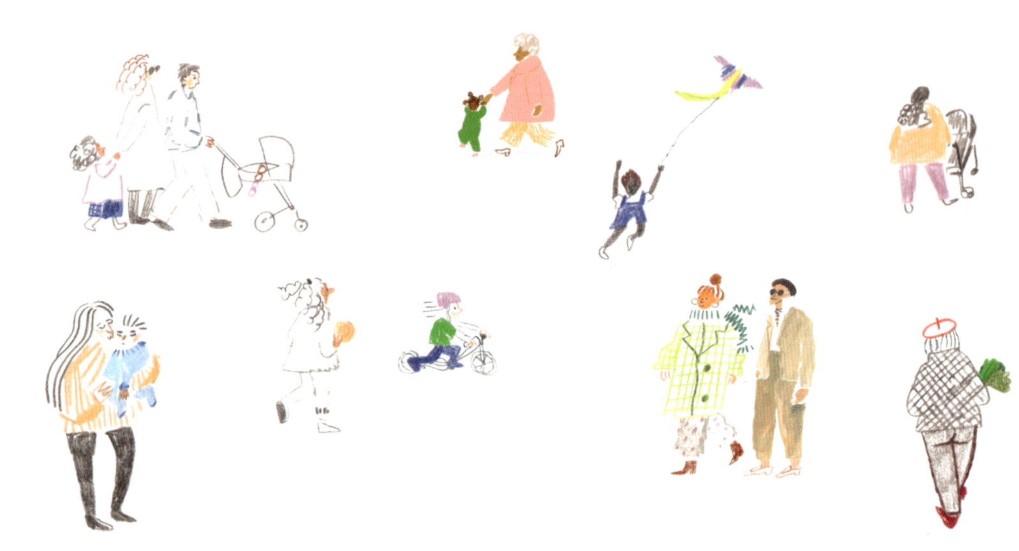

DRAW A PARK IN THIS SPACE AND GET INSPIRED BY THE TONAL GUIDELINES.

Draw some people and see if that adds another dynamic and some movement to your park landscape.

ADD AN ANIMAL, INSECT OR VEGETATION TO THESE ABSTRACT SHAPES AND SEE HOW THIS CHANGES HOW YOU PERCEIVE THAT OBJECT.

Is it now a large rock next to a teeny tiny ant, a huge tree next to an elephant or a tiny patch of moss next to a dog's paw? Create your own abstract shapes and then add an animal to them.

SEE HOW ADDING ANOTHER ELEMENT TO THE ABSTRACT SHAPES CHANGES THE DRAWINGS. TRY ADDING LITTLE PEOPLE TO MATCH TOO.

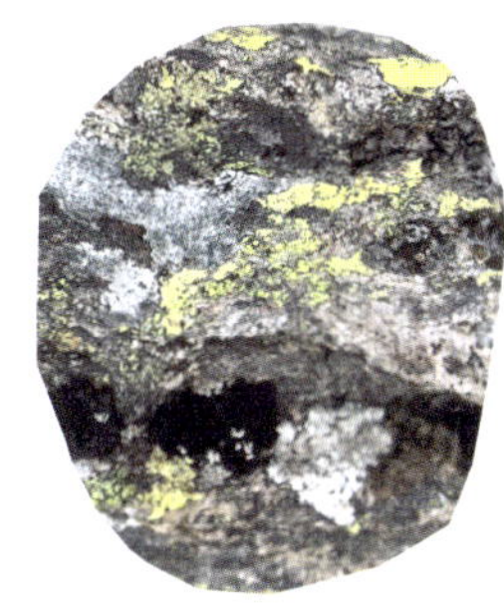

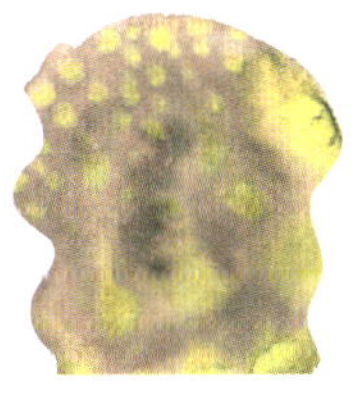

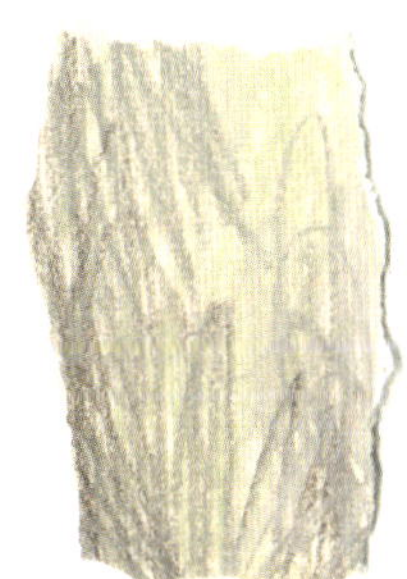

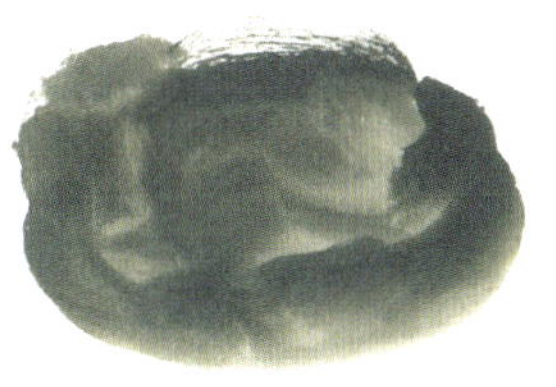

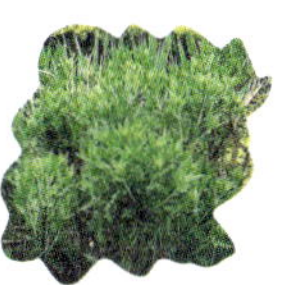

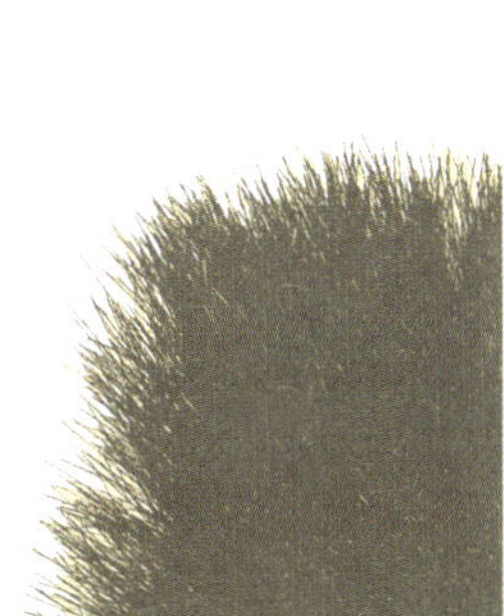

LINEAR PERSPECTIVE

Linear perspective is a technique used to create the illusion of depth and space on a flat surface. Using this perspective, if we continue drawing the parallel sides, they would converge at a single vanishing point on the horizon.

The vanishing point on the table below is at the top of the vase of flowers. Let's try to recreate this table scene on the right-hand page, using the guidelines provided.

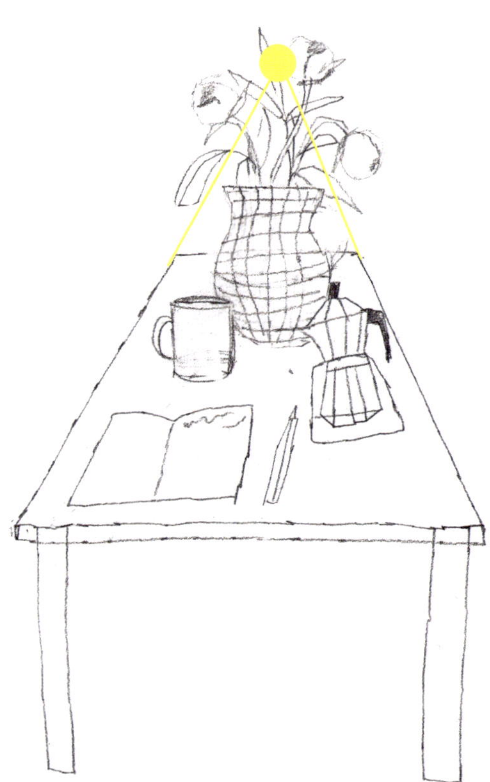

AXONOMETRIC PERSPECTIVE

There are no vanishing points in the drawings below. Rather the objects appear in such a way that you can see three sides of them at the same time. Your eye can wander around the objects. Using the guidlines opposite, draw your own axonometric scene (for example, your drawing table, a room with some plants or a local park). Think of an old-school game graphics or a miniature city with a park which you can overlook slightly from above. This method of drawing allows you to add many details to the setting.

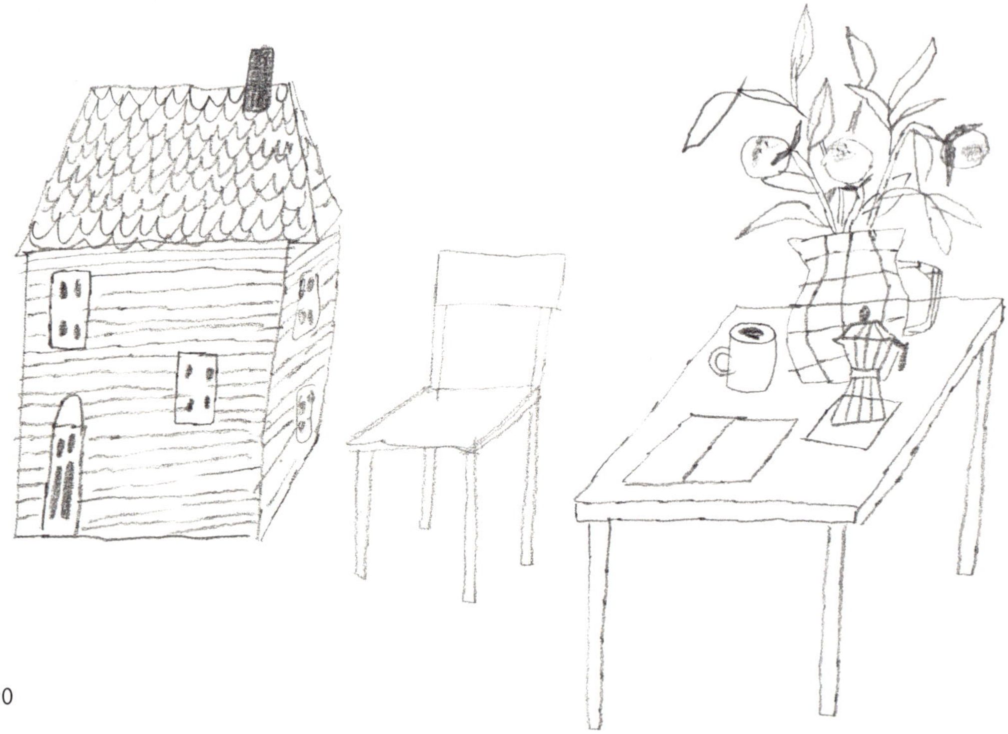

REVERSE PERSPECTIVE

Here, you, the viewer, are the vanishing point and all of the parallel lines diverge towards you. This perspective creates a sense of intimacy and adds a really interesting element to the environment. Try it for yourself in the space opposite. You could draw a house, table – anything at all.

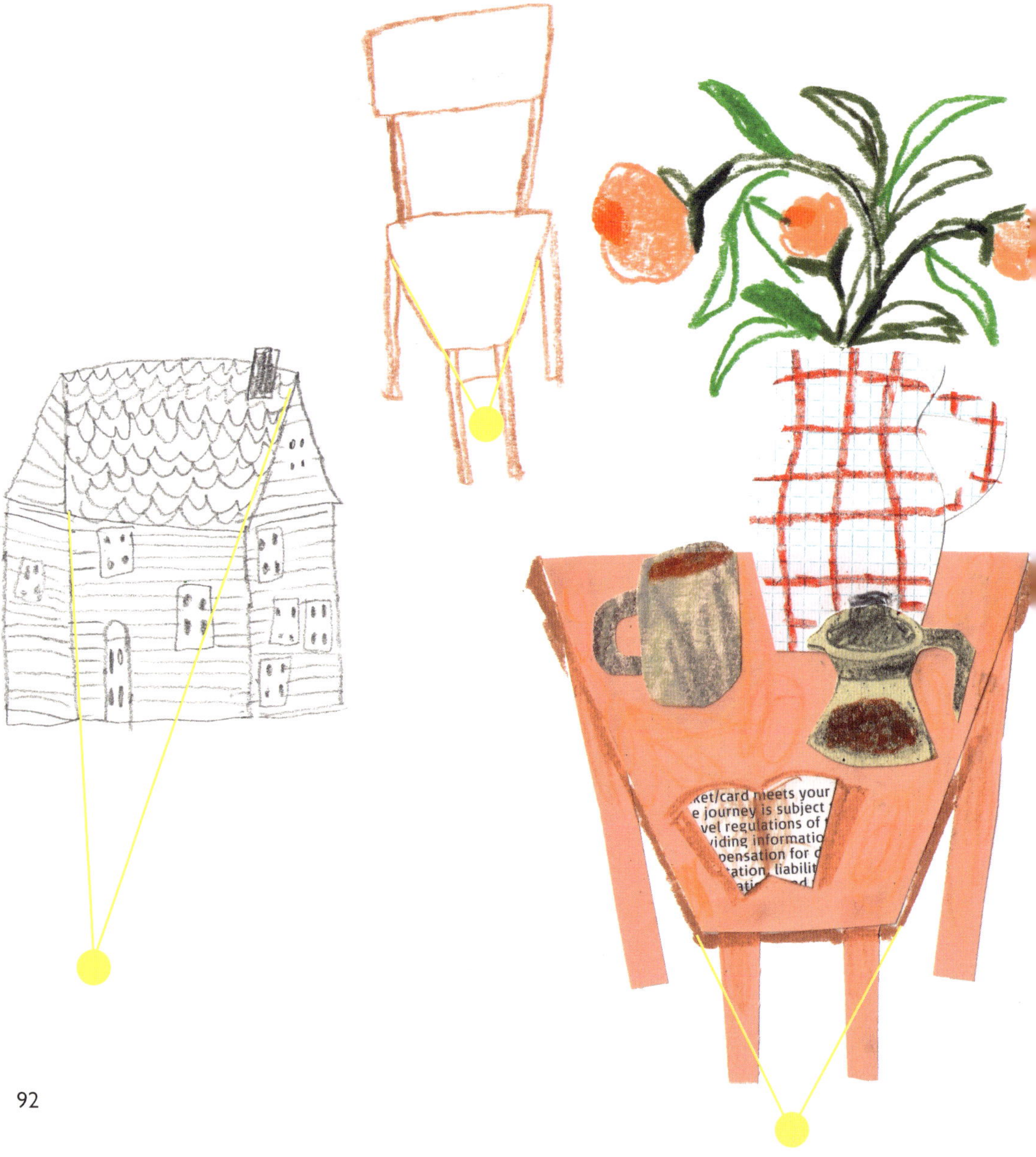

ORTHOGRAPHIC PERSPECTIVE

Orthographic perspective is a single, two-dimensional view of an object. Let's it try for ourselves! Copy the objects I have drawn or have a go at drawing your own.

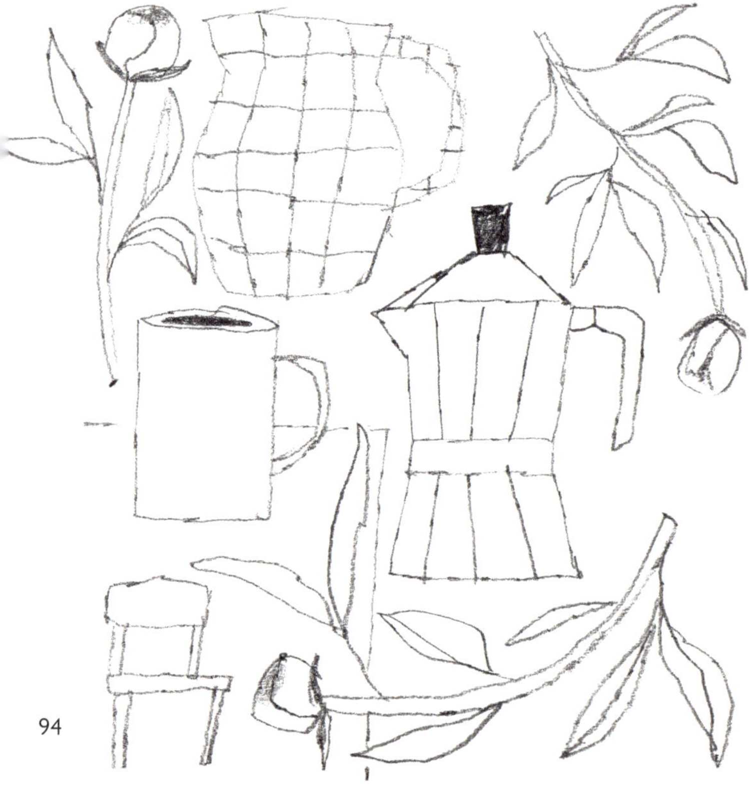

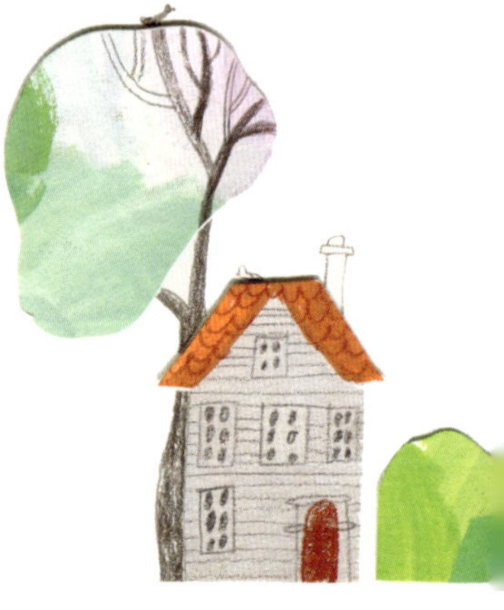

DRAW MORE BIRDS ON THE LAKE, NESTING IN THE TREES OR FLYING ABOVE THE PEOPLE WALKING.

Use any materials you like!

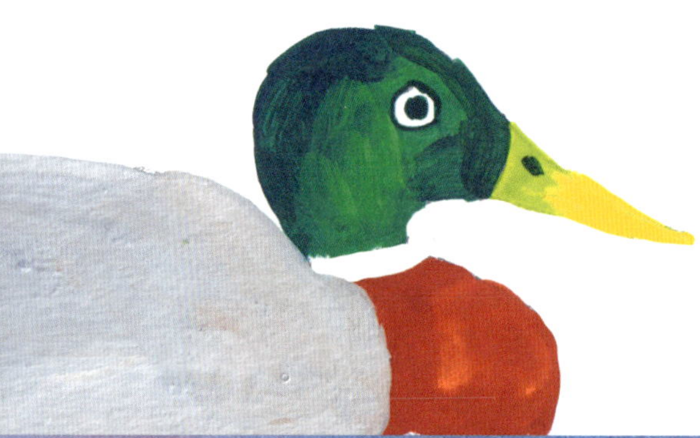

DRAW A LARGE FLOCK OF STARLINGS AS THEY FLY TOGETHER ACROSS THE EVENING SKY.

Use a dark colouring pencil or similar and make playful marks to emulate the birds as they change direction.

DRAW A FOREST BELOW THESE FLYING BIRDS.

Make the woodland 3D or 2D and draw trees, bushes, flowers and open spaces for picnics. Add more flying birds, too, if you like.

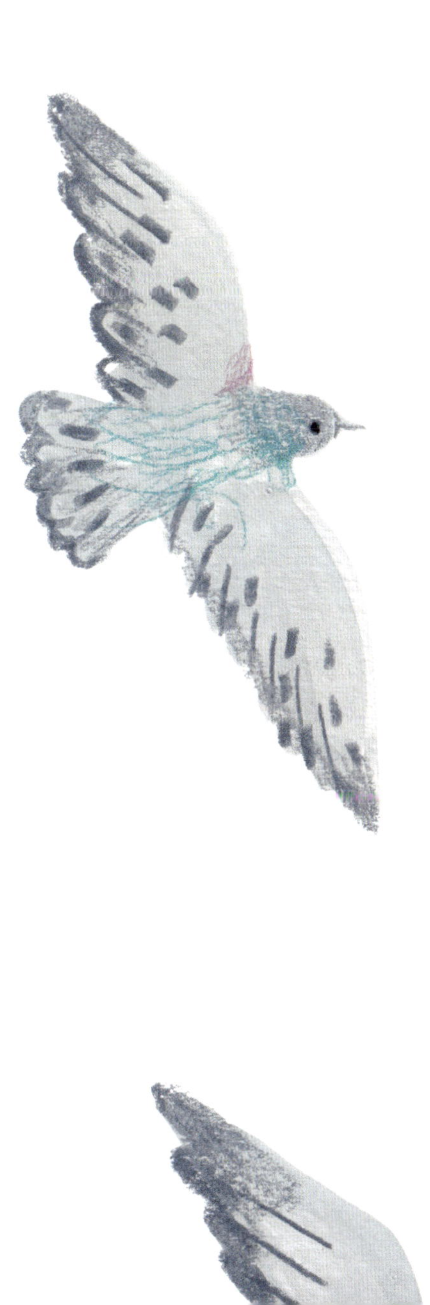

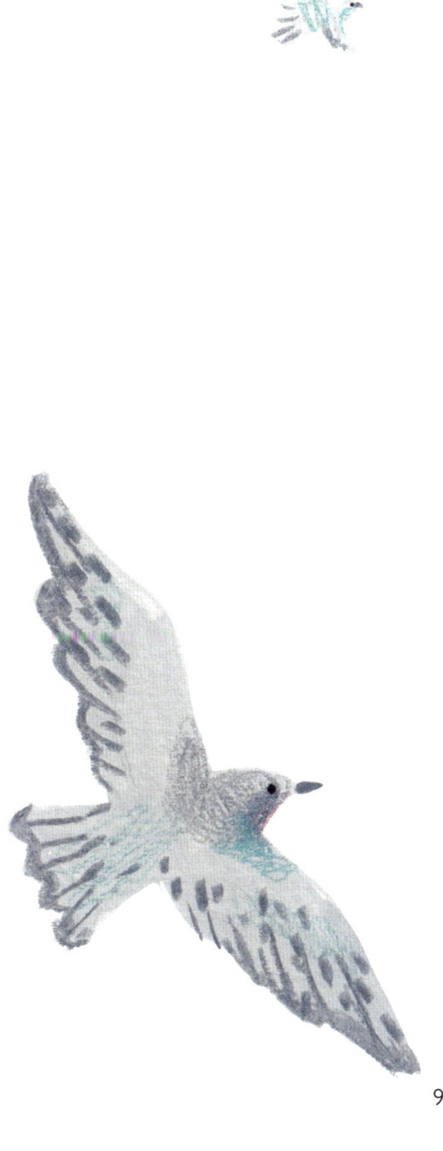

DRAW YOUR NEIGHBOURHOOD USING ORTHOGRAPHIC PERSPECTIVE, WHERE ALL OBJECTS ARE IN 2D.

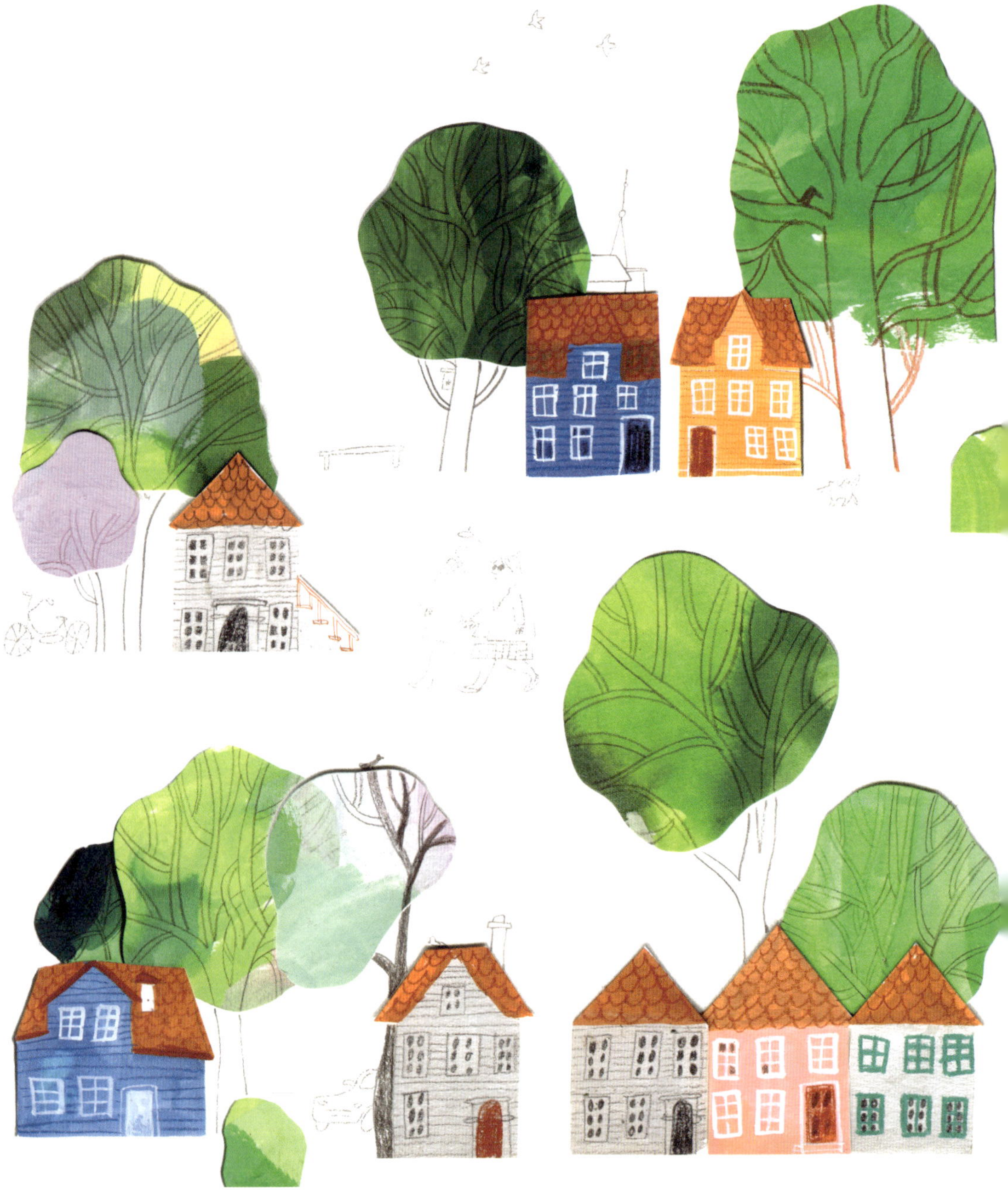

CREATE YOUR OWN TAPESTRY TO SHOWCASE YOUR LATEST ADVENTURE, WALK OR EVEN HOLIDAY!

Stylise shapes, play around with scale and include important and fun details. Feature animals you saw, landscapes, fruit, trees, birds, etc.

IN SOME CULTURES, PEOPLE DON'T SEE THEIR SURROUNDING AREAS AS BELONGING TO THEM INSTEAD, THEY BELONG TO THEIR SURROUNDS.

Do you belong to a mountain, a lake, a tree? Draw your inner landscape here.

DRAW YOUR LOCAL TOWN, VILLAGE OR CITY AS A MAP.

Include your favourite places to visit!

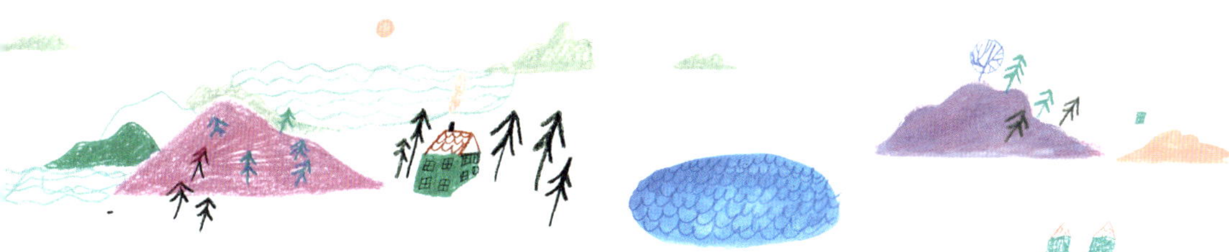

AERIAL PERSPECTIVE IS A GREAT WAY TO COMMUNICATE DISTANCE AND DEPTH IN YOUR DRAWING.

There are a few techniques to achieve this and you can mix and match them in your drawings. Try for yourself here!

TONES

Objects closer to you will be higher in value (darker) and have higher contrast. Objects further away will be lower in value (lighter) and have lower contrast.

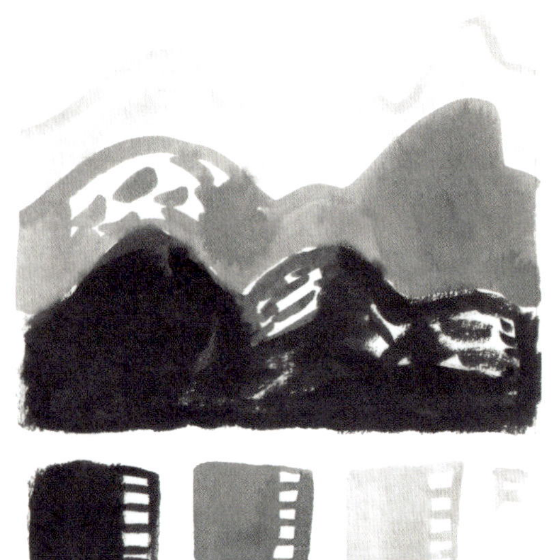

COLOUR

Objects closer to you will be more saturated and objects further away will be less saturated and brighter in tonal value (adding some dark colour or black and white to the colours will help with achieving that effect). I especially love adding purple and dark green to the mix to achieve this.

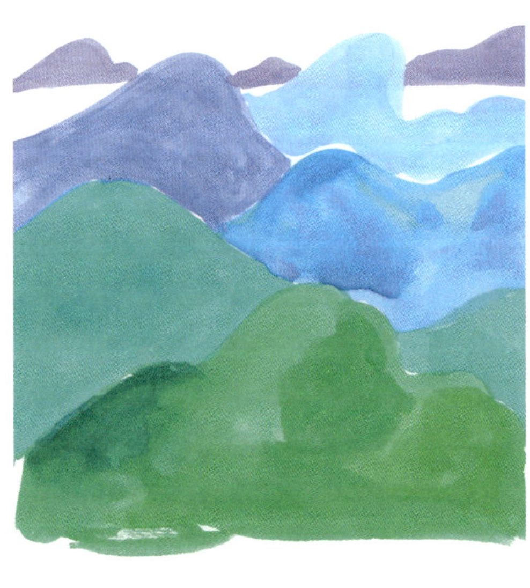

MARK MAKING

Marks closer to you will be more defined, bigger and bolder. They will become smaller, softer and less defined the further away the object is.

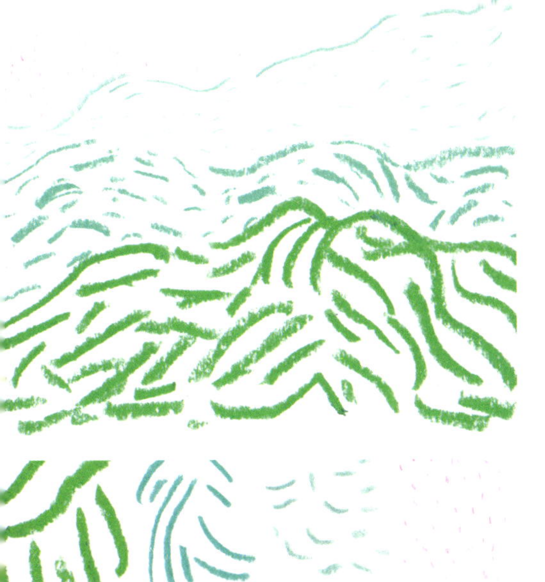

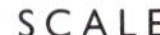

SCALE

Objects closer to you are bigger and objects further away are smaller. It's a wonderful, rhythmical solution for communicating distance.

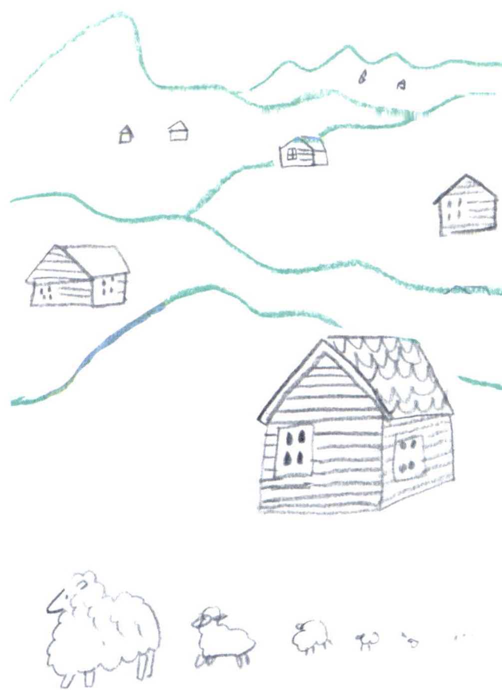

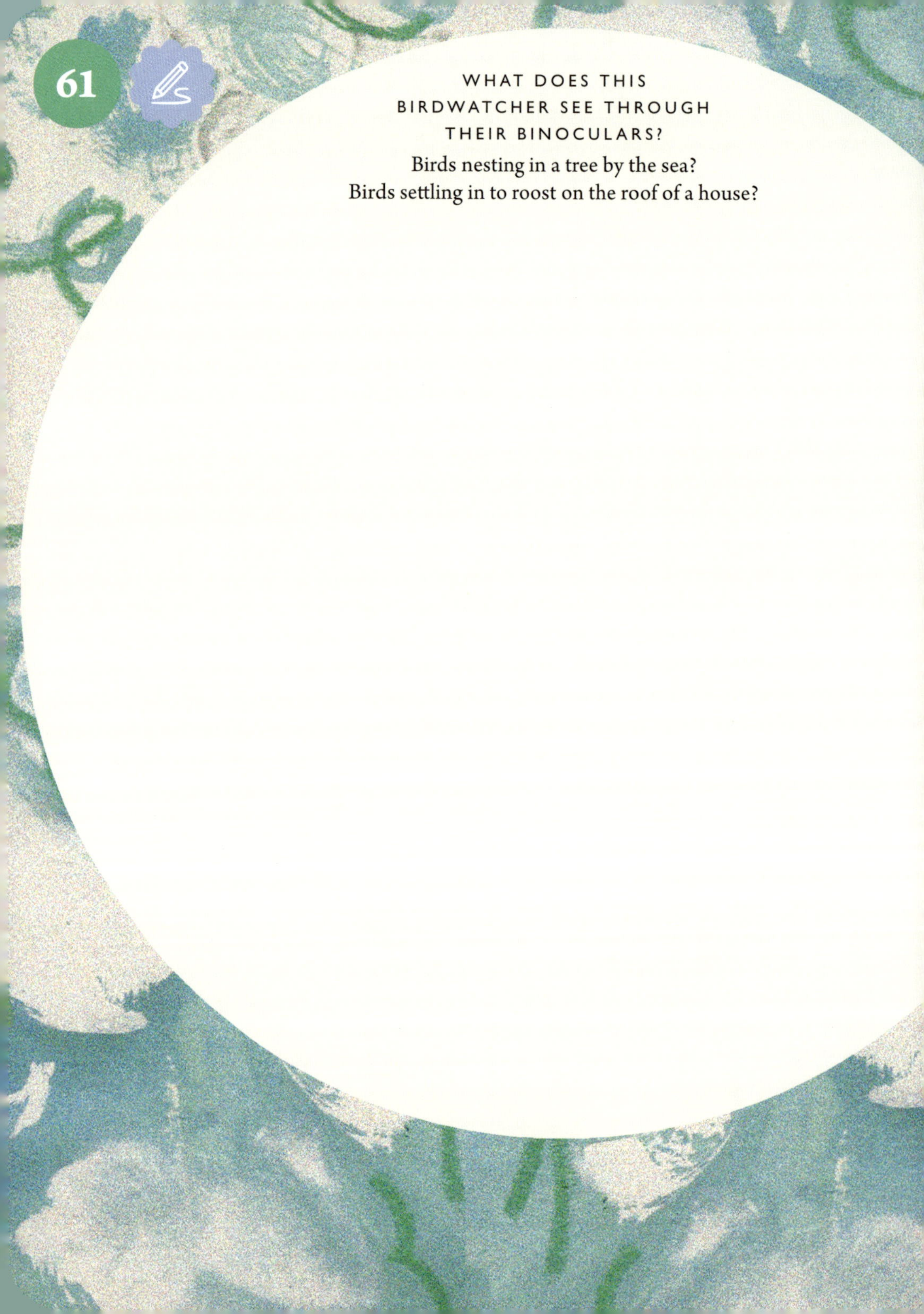

61

WHAT DOES THIS BIRDWATCHER SEE THROUGH THEIR BINOCULARS?

Birds nesting in a tree by the sea?
Birds settling in to roost on the roof of a house?

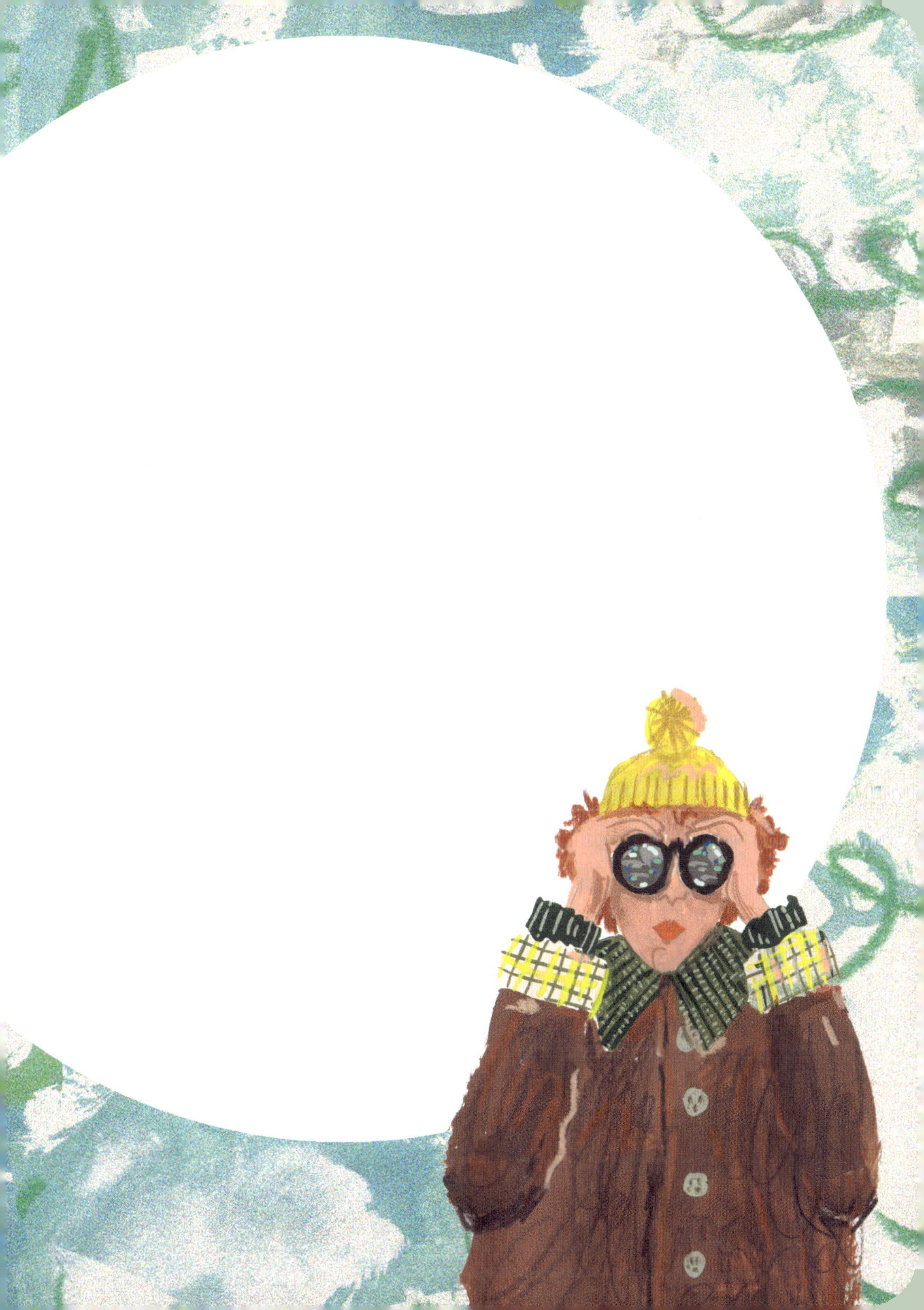

LET'S CREATE A VISUAL DIARY OF THE LAST WALK YOU TOOK!

Fill the squares using the following prompts:

A CLOSE-UP OF AN INSECT

FLORA OR FAUNA YOU SAW

A BIRD OR AN ANIMAL

YOUR FAVOURITE VIEW

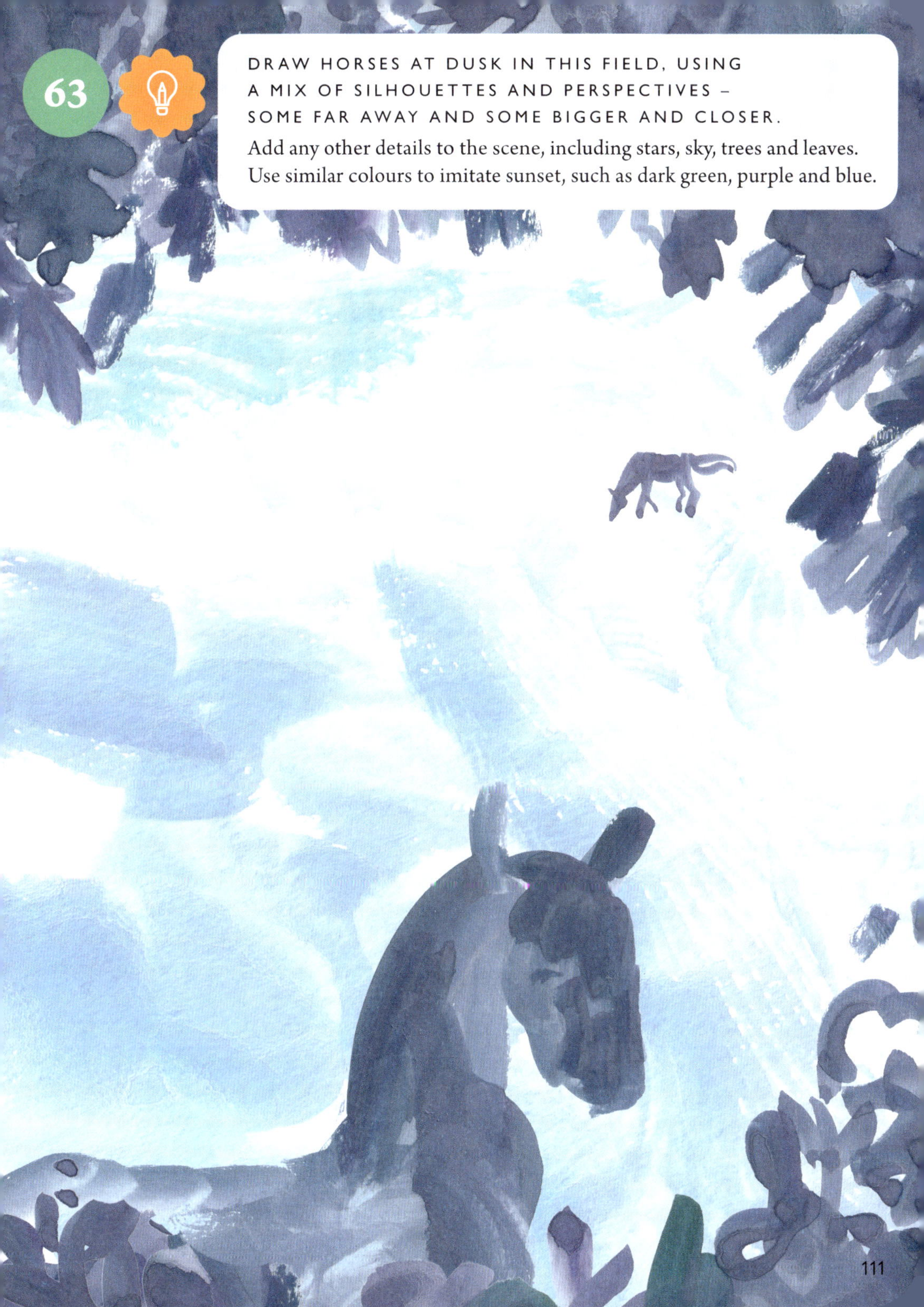

63

DRAW HORSES AT DUSK IN THIS FIELD, USING A MIX OF SILHOUETTES AND PERSPECTIVES – SOME FAR AWAY AND SOME BIGGER AND CLOSER.

Add any other details to the scene, including stars, sky, trees and leaves. Use similar colours to imitate sunset, such as dark green, purple and blue.

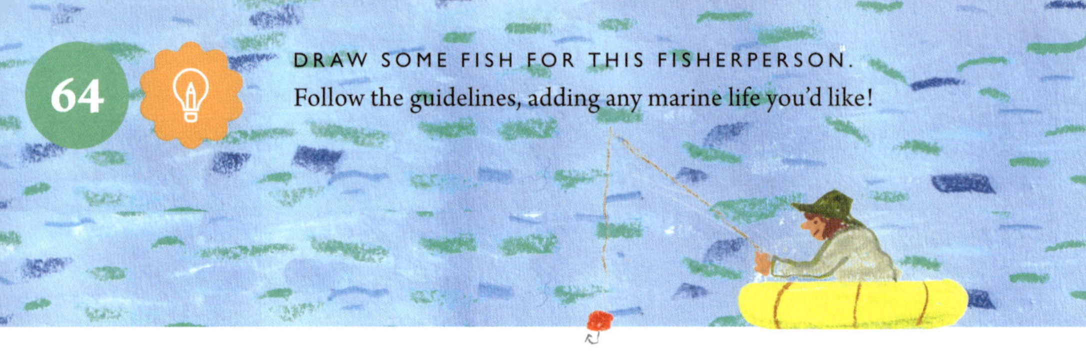
64
DRAW SOME FISH FOR THIS FISHERPERSON.
Follow the guidelines, adding any marine life you'd like!

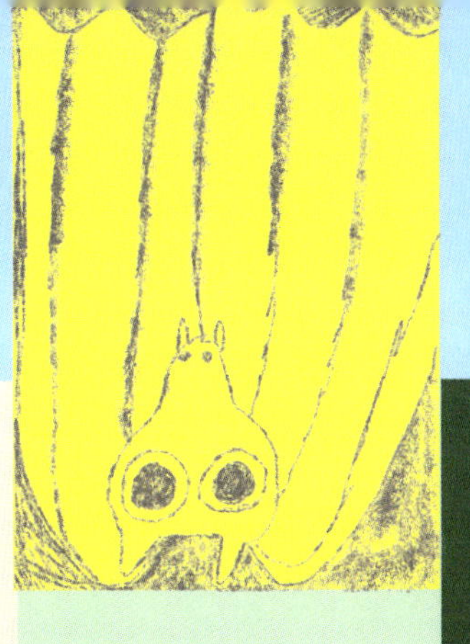

USING A GRAPHITE PENCIL, DRAW DIFFERENT ANIMALS AND MAKE THEM FIT TIGHTLY INTO THESE COLOURFUL SHAPES.

FILL THIS PAGE WITH AS MANY DIFFERENT SKIES AS POSSIBLE.

Create a variety of weather patterns – rain, clouds, storms, clear skies and sunsets – and think about the textures and materials that could help you achieve the different skies.

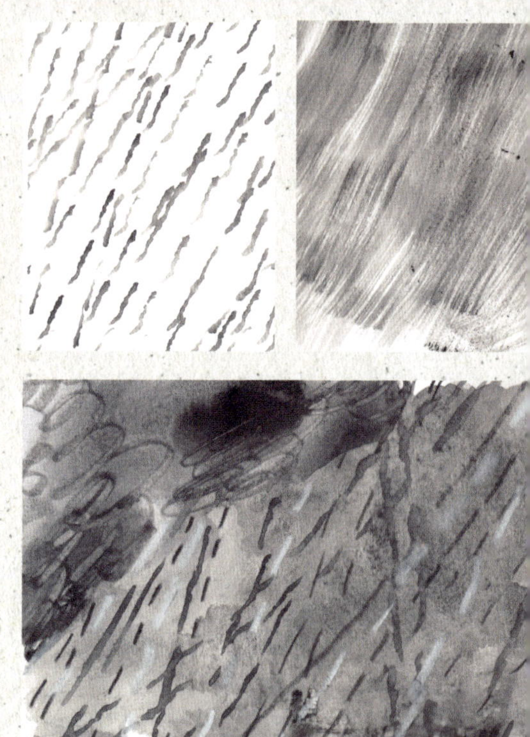

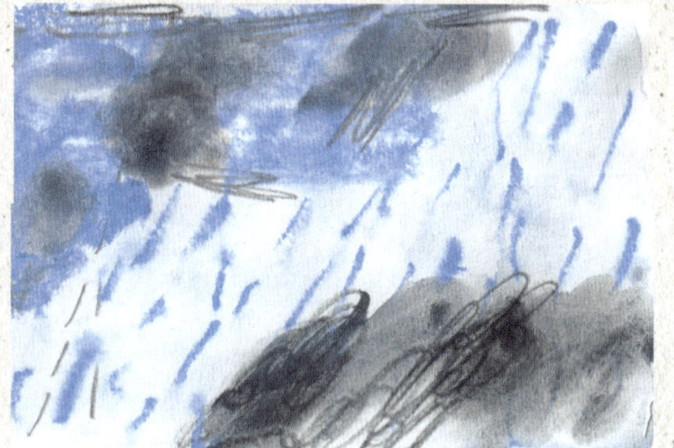

WHAT'S YOUR FAVOURITE FLOWER?

Mine has to be hydrangeas!
Draw your favourite flower!

DRAW A SELF-PORTRAIT
WITH A BEAUTIFUL AND LUSH
BOUQUET FEATURING SOME
OF YOUR FAVOURITE FLOWERS!

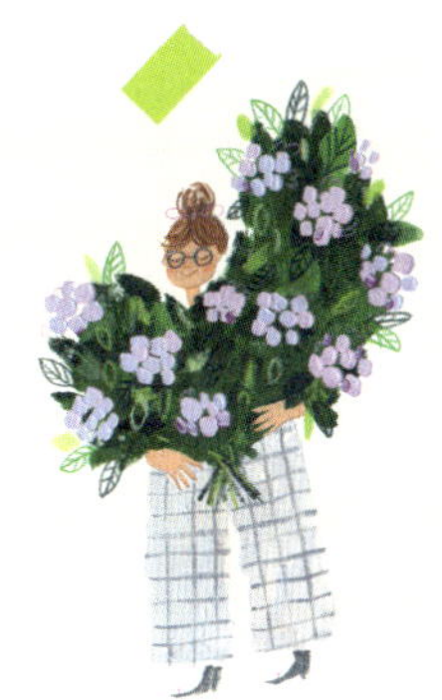

FLORAL STEP-BY-STEP

MATERIALS:
A4 or A5 sheet of paper
Paper to test your colours
Graphite pencil
Paintbrushes
Paint
Colouring pencils, marker pens or fine liners
Water

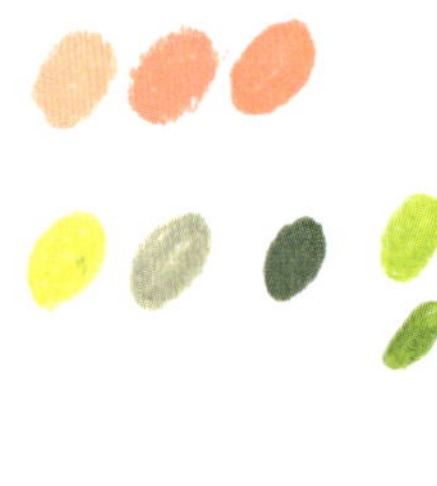

STEP 1

Using a graphite pencil, sketch your composition. I placed some rhododendron flowers in the foreground, people in the middle and more flowers in the background.

STEP 2

Now let's create a background wash with a paintbrush. I used a light pistachio green to cover the majority of my artwork to reflect the greenery. Then, I added apricot to highlight aspects of the drawing, including a flower in the foreground, the people walking through the scene and some flowers in the background. Go light with the background colour as we will continue building on it later.

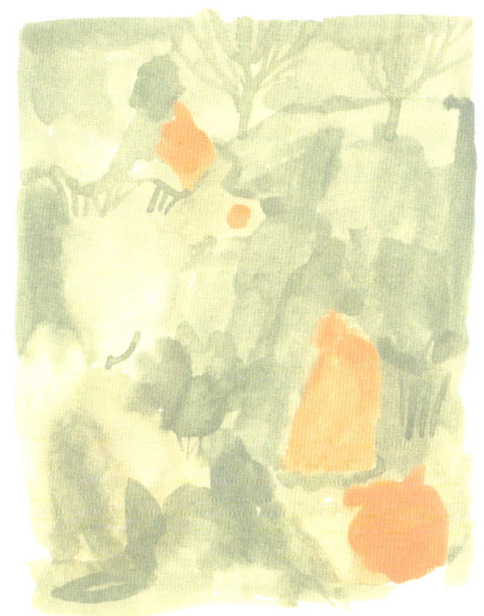

STEP 3

Using a dark green colouring pencil or other tool of your choice, draw the leaves of the rhododendron as well as other flowers in the foreground. Mix a mid-green using green paint and, to create a softer line, paint some more flowers in the middle ground. Think of the atmospheric perspective rules. Saturated and high contrast in the foreground and softer, less contrasted in the background.

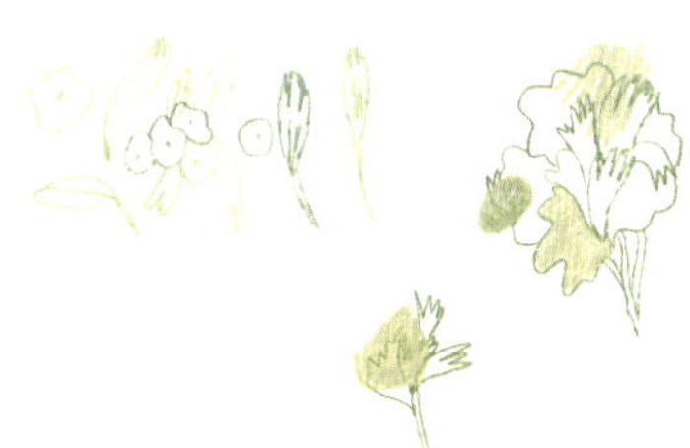

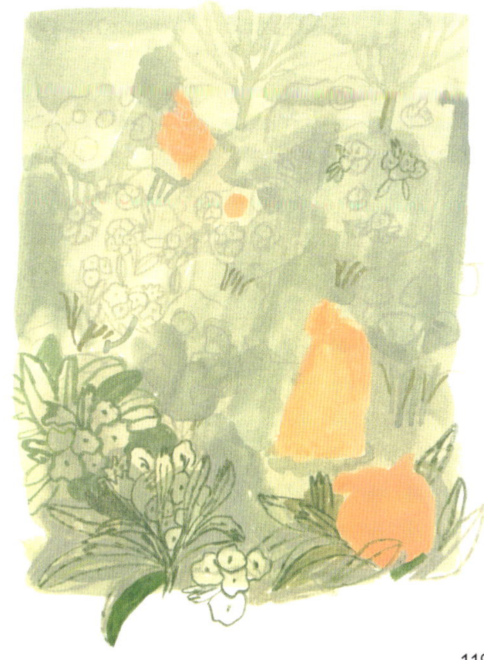

STEP 4

Returning to the background, add a light wash of pistachio paint around the flowers. Make the pistachio a little darker and paint around the bushes and flowers in the middle ground.

Using the same pistachio wash as you did for the background, lightly paint around the people, adding marks to create foliage.

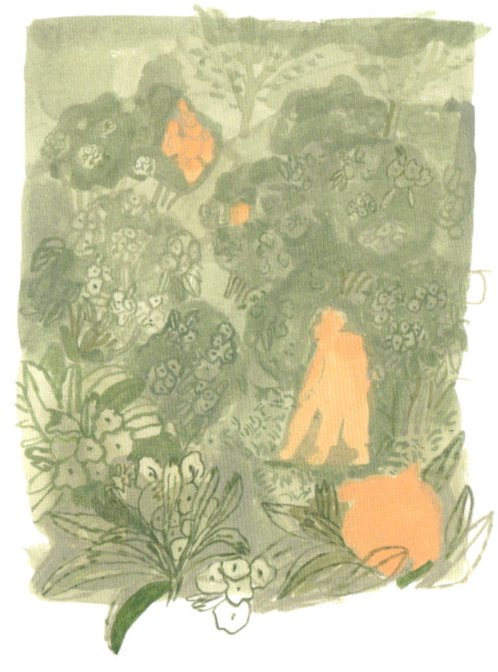

STEP 5

Using the dark green paint, add details to the people, including facial features, clothes, etc. Build on the apricot elements by adding marks, shadows and texture using a dark green colouring pencil, marker pen or fine liner. Add blooms and leaves to the rhododendron, darken the details on the people and to create shadows underneath them.

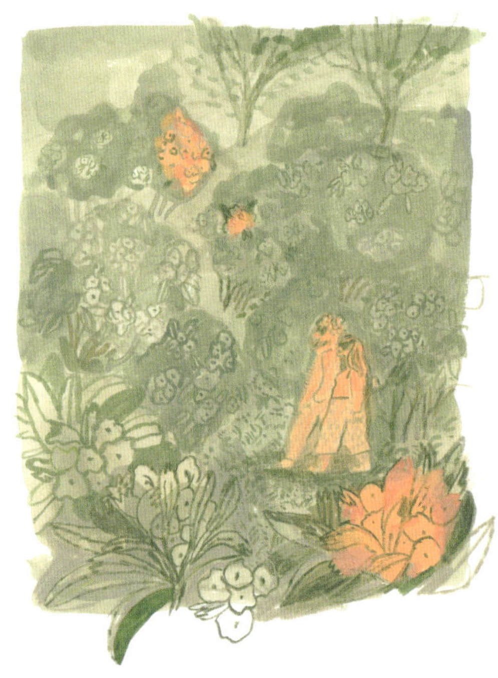

STEP 6

With a lime-green or lemon-yellow pencil or other tool, fill in some of the leaves and flowers to add a pop of colour. You can also use this colour in places you feel need a bit more balance, including around the people and apricot flowers in the background! Add blue to create a glimpse of sky in the top-left corner.

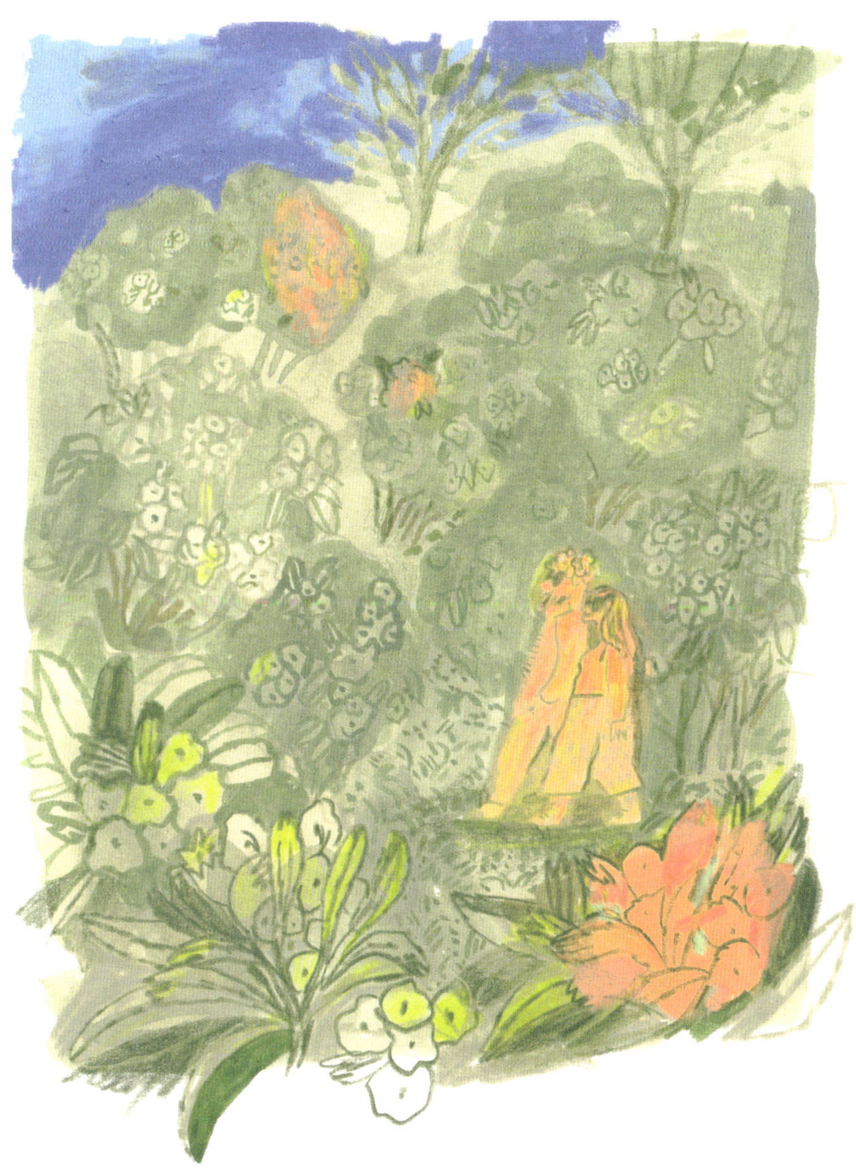

DRAW THE SAME LANDSCAPE DURING DIFFERENT SEASONS.

I've drawn a tree, but you could try a view from your window or a local park.

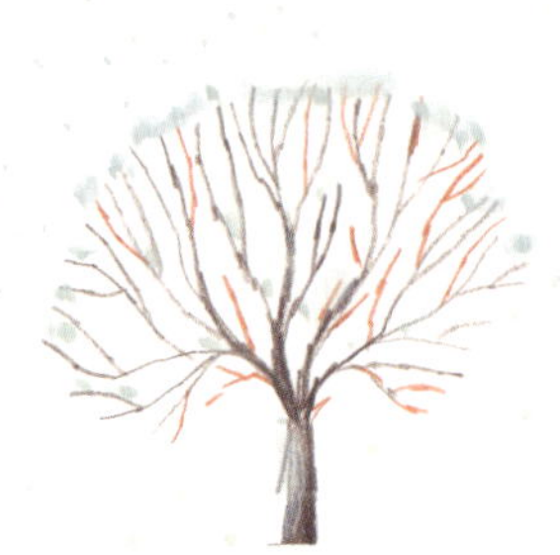

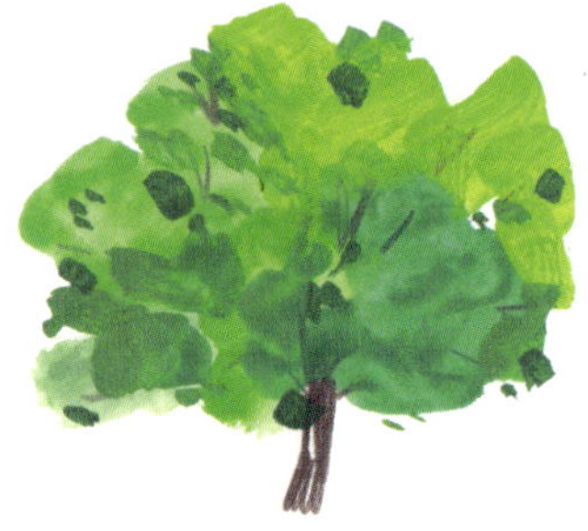

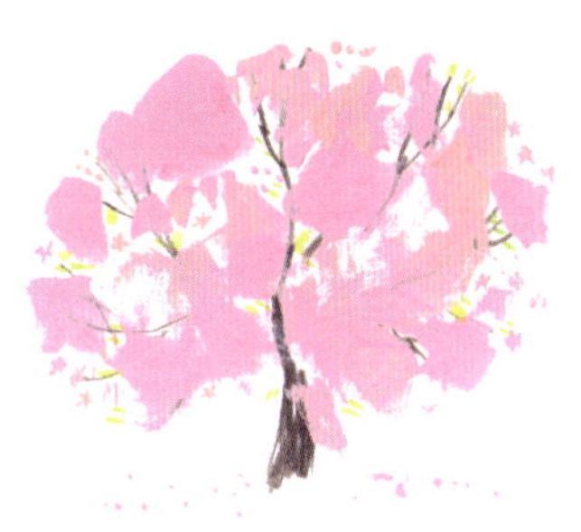

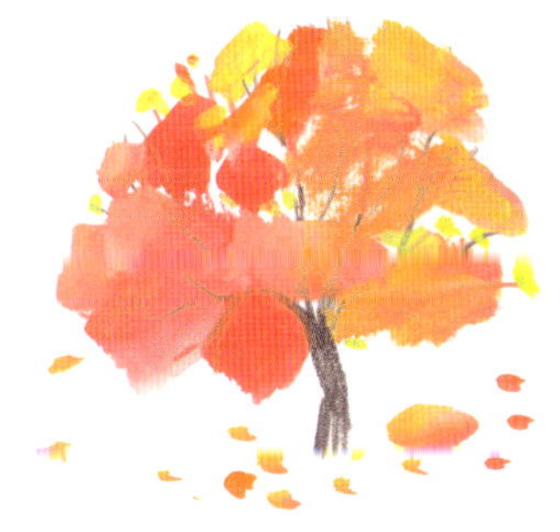

ONE OF THE BEST WAYS TO LOOSEN UP YOUR STYLE AND REIGNITE YOUR CREATIVITY IS TO SWITCH UP THE TOOLS YOU USE.

Especially if they force you to work bolder and braver. Use a new drawing tool to create as many wild and free marks as you can here.

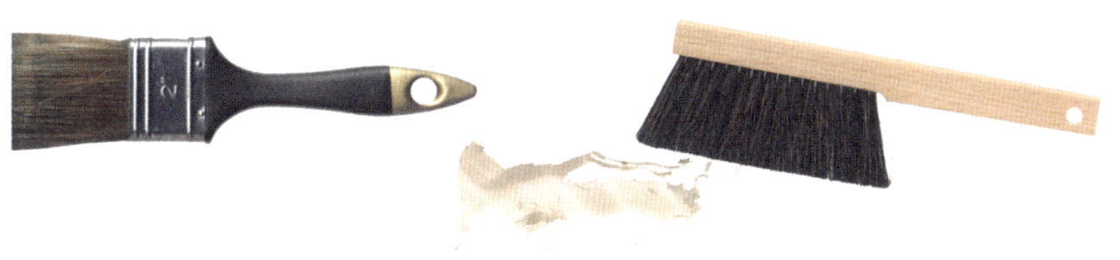

DRAW TREES, PARKS, BUTTERFLIES AND BIRDS TO BRING NATURE INTO THIS URBAN ENVIRONMENT.

Follow the guidelines or design your own town! Add squirrels, flower-beds – whatever you'd like to bring some greenery to your town!

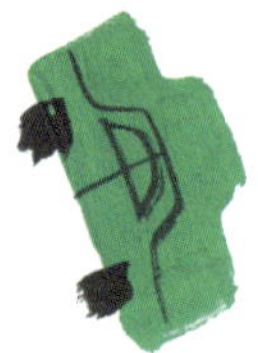

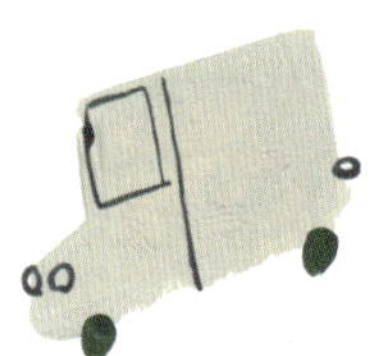

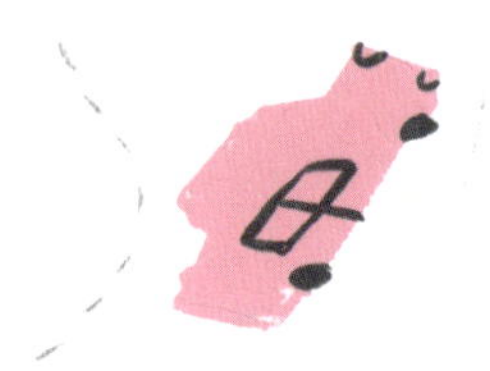

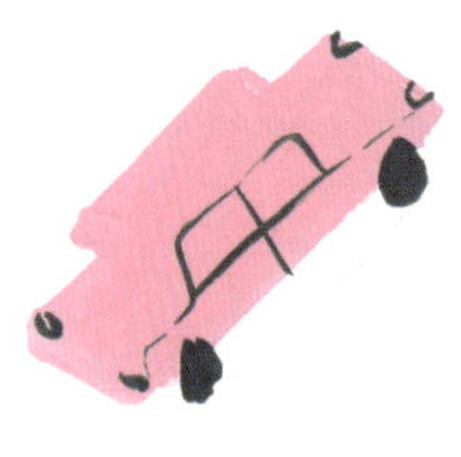

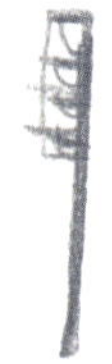

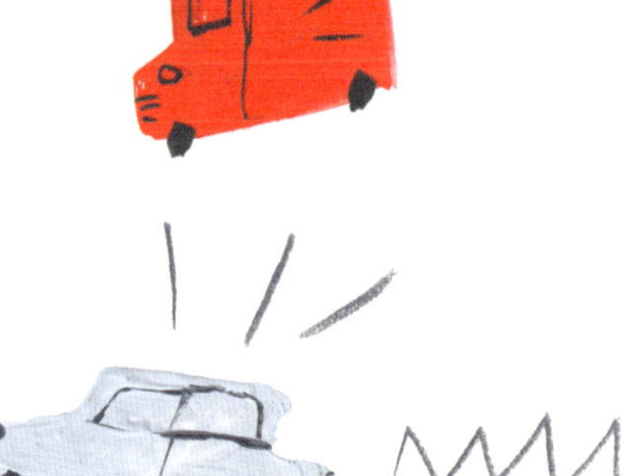

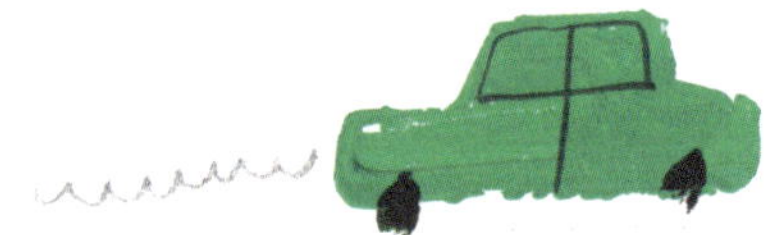

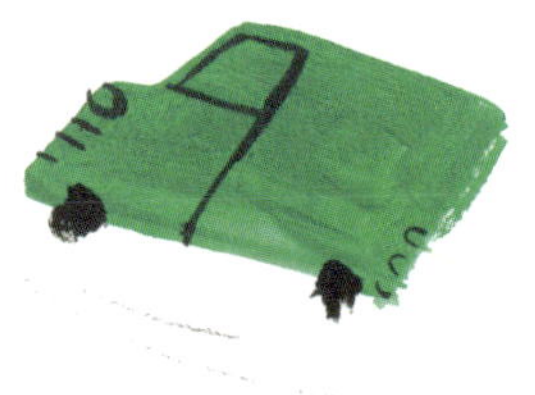

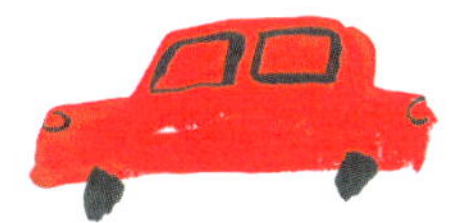
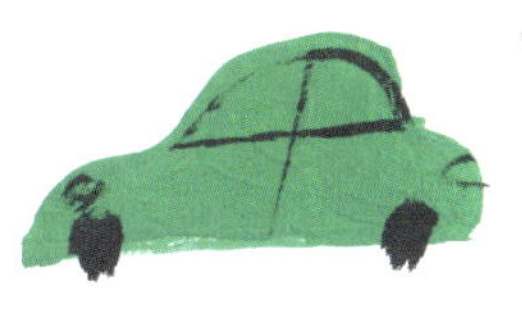
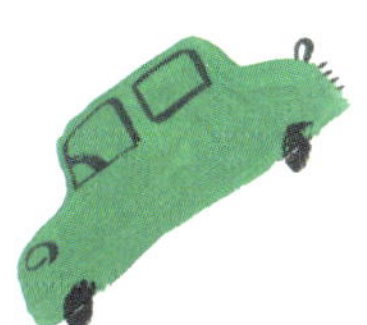
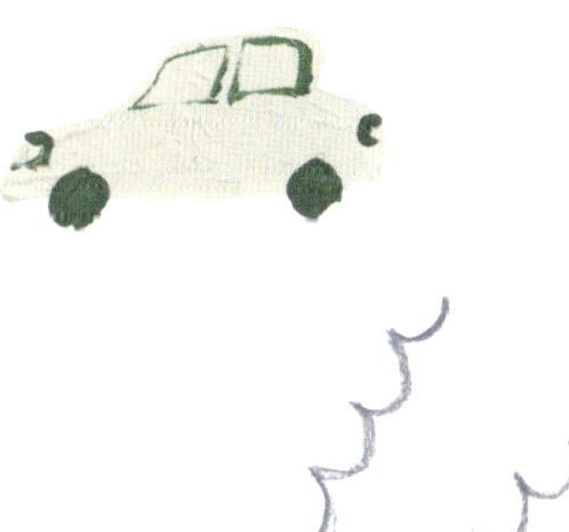
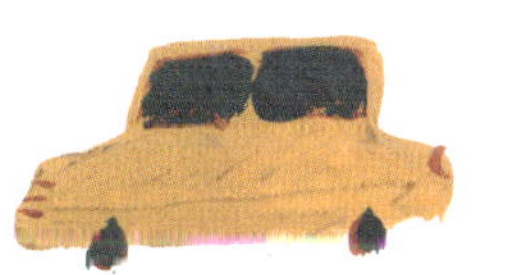
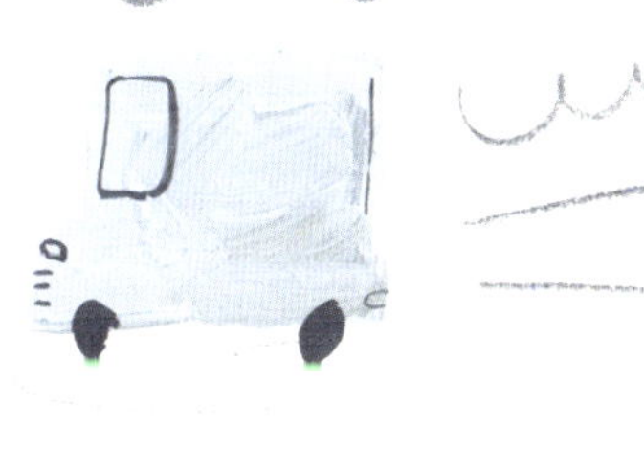
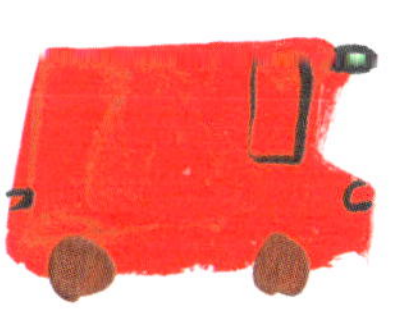
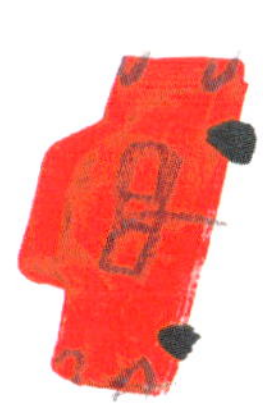
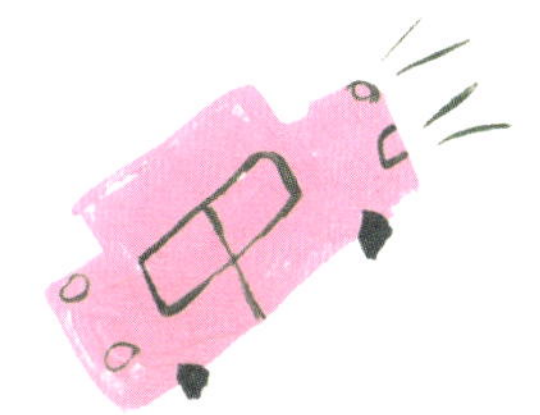
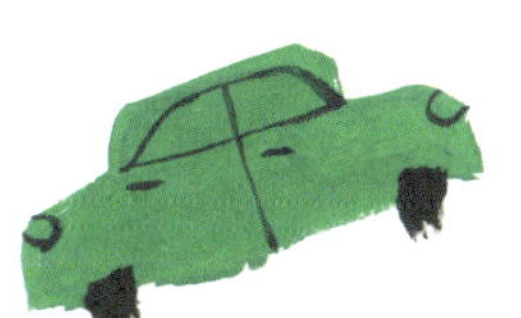

WE CAN USE RHYTHM AS A TOOL IN DRAWING TO COMMUNICATE DISTANCE, REPETITION AND MOVEMENT.

Fill this page with different water flows, thinking about how they all move. How would it look if you drew a waterfall versus a puddle, raindrops falling into the water, a tap on maximum, a fountain, a stagnant pond, etc?

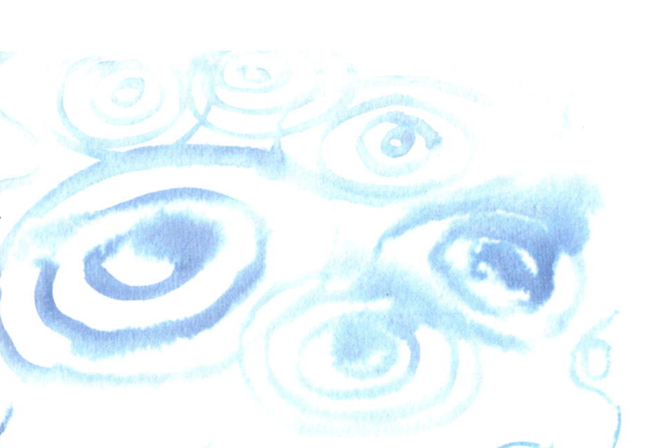

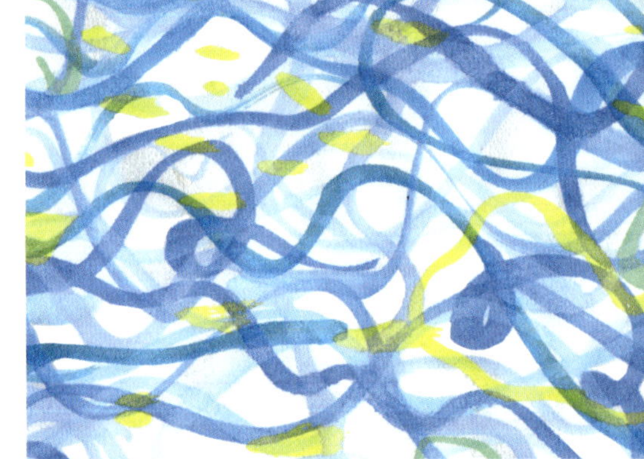

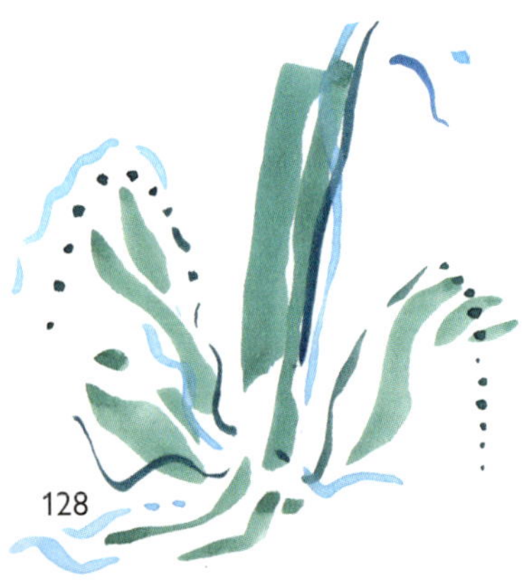

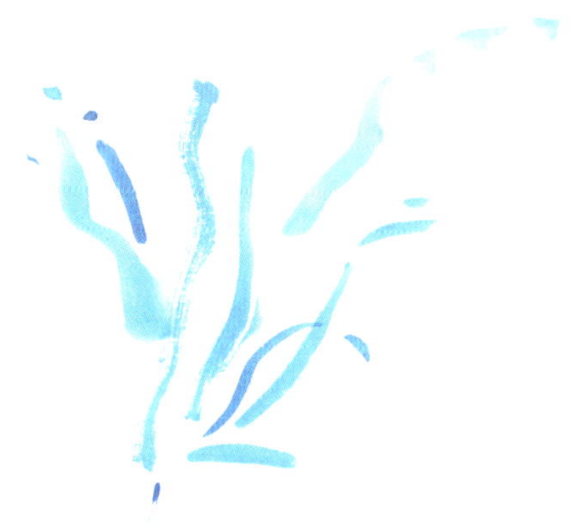

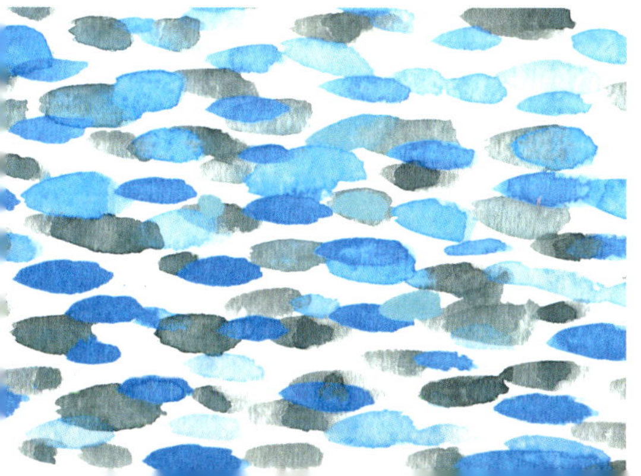

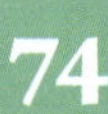

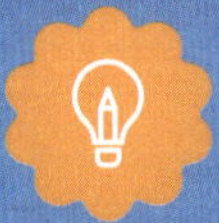

DRAW A LAKE REFLECTION FOR THIS MOUNTAIN LANDSCAPE

Play with different ways to communicate the movement of the water – will there be ripples, waves or is it still a lake?

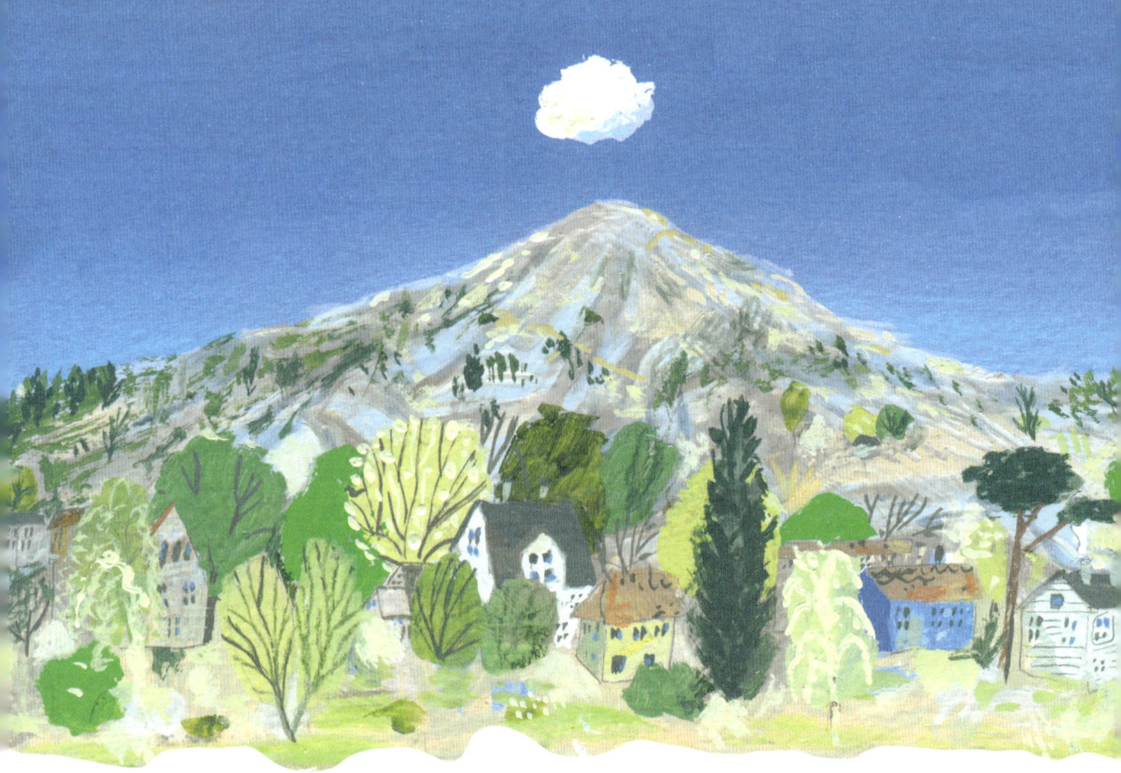

DRAW YOUR OWN LANDSCAPE NEXT TO A LAKE, RIVER OR SEA AND THEN DRAW THE REFLECTION.

DRAW YOUR HAPPY PLACE.

It could be a garden, a view from the window or a childhood memory of a place. For me, it's a tiny lake, not far from where I live. With a beautiful red hut just next to it.

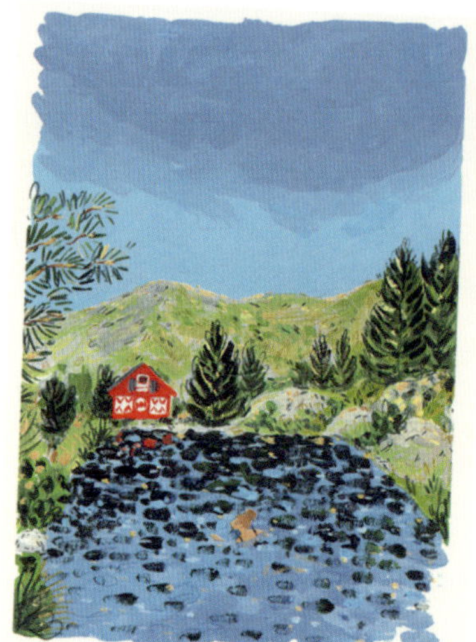

LET'S EXPERIMENT WITH COLOUR.

Choose any four colours and a simple motif, like a flower, and create four variations by rearranging the colours.

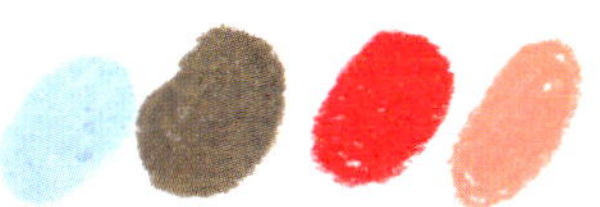

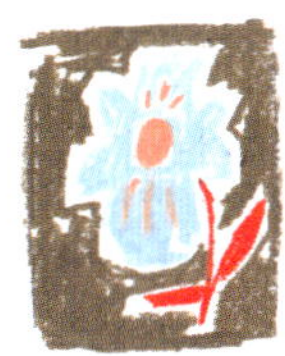

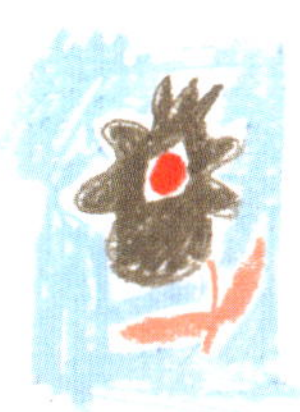

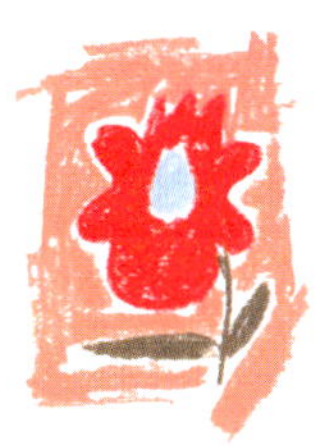

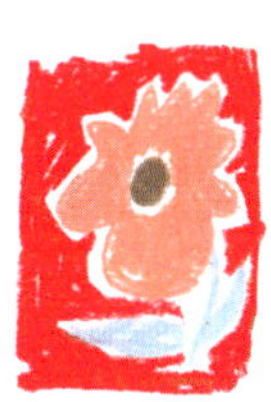

ONE OF MY FAVOURITE VISUAL METHODS IS COMBINING A FULLY FILLED-IN COLOUR BACKGROUND WITH JUST OUTLINES FOR THE SUBJECTS AND THE SURROUNDINGS.

It gives the drawing a fun rhythm and an interesting atmosphere. Fill in this page with a scene, maybe an open-air café in the park, or perhaps boats and birds on a lake – you decide. But draw your subjects and setting in outlines!

DRAW ROCKS AND MINERALS IN THESE SQUARES.

Experiment with colours and textures, overlay, mark make and have lots of fun.

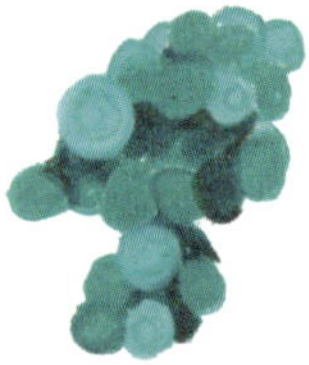

JUXTAPOSING ELEMENTS DRAWN AT DIFFERENT SCALES IS A FUN WAY TO MAKE THE COMPOSITION MORE INTERESTING AND HIGHLIGHT THE SIZE OF BOTH SUBJECTS.

Draw a tiny house next to a large mountain (or replace the mountain with an ocean, giant tree, field etc.)

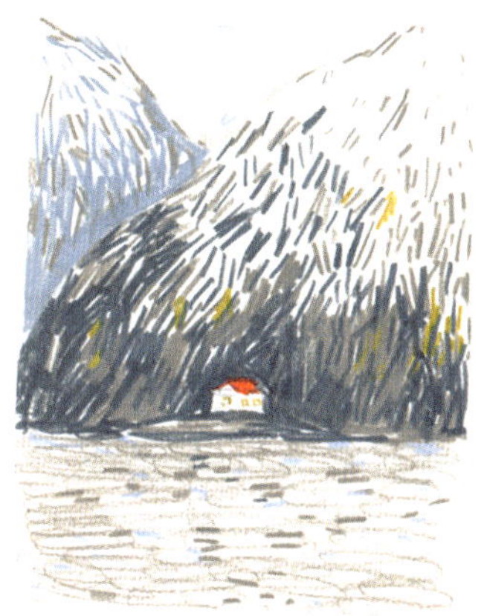

USING ONE COLOUR, DRAW AS MANY TREE SHAPES AS YOU CAN.

Play around and experiment here, starting each drawing rooted in reality and then allowing yourself to be carried away with play, lines and abstract shapes! How far can you push the drawing of a tree?

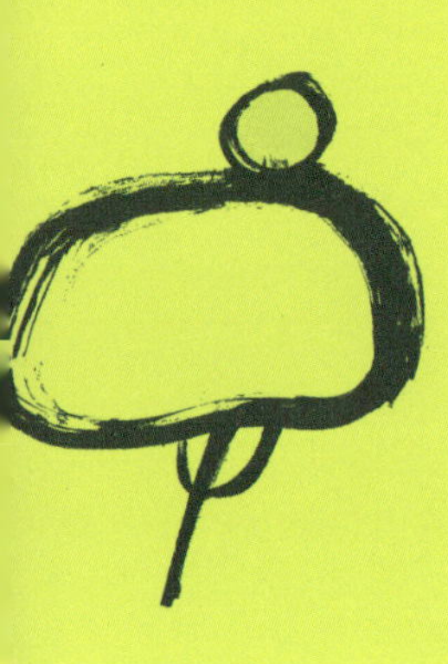

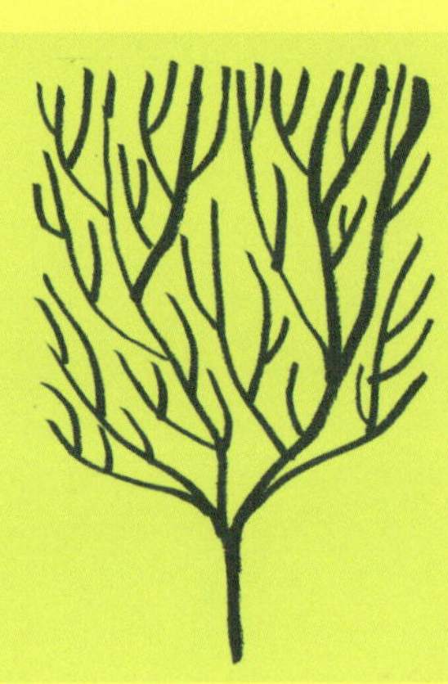

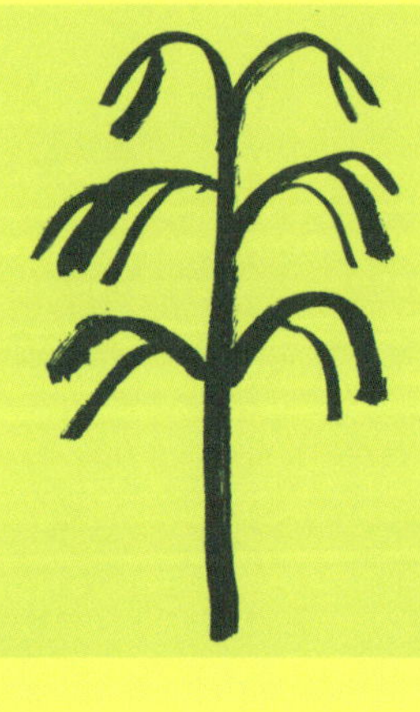

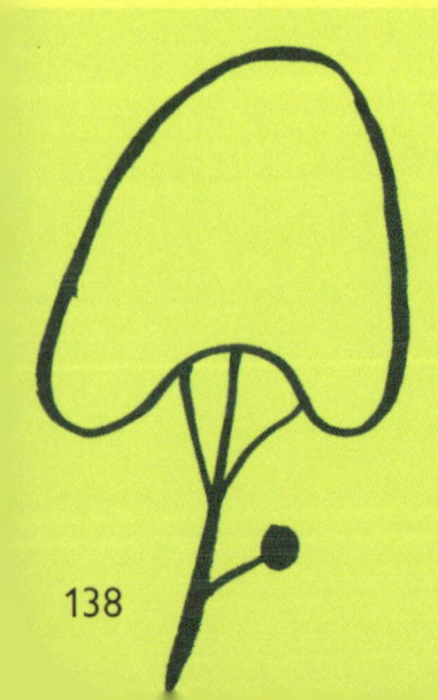

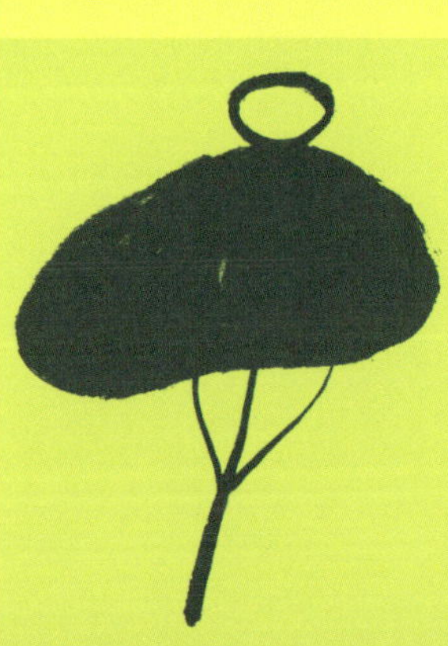

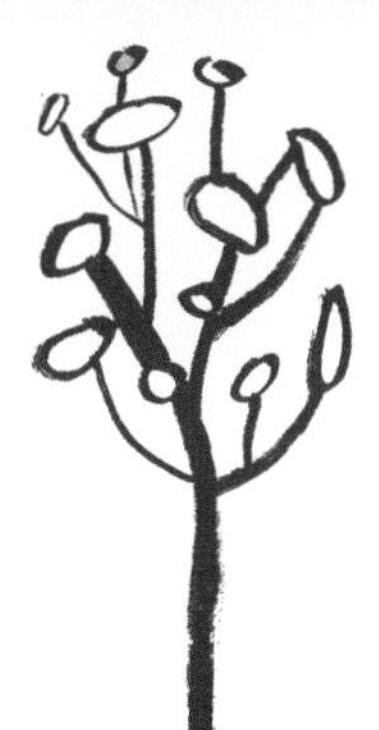

DRAW A WINTER LANDSCAPE USING THE WHITE OF THE PAPER AS PART OF YOUR PICTURE – SNOW IN THIS CASE.

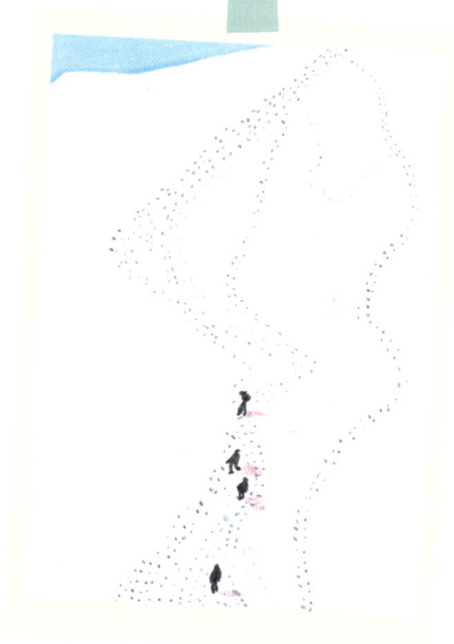

PLACE YOURSELF SOMEWHERE YOU CAN LISTEN TO THE SOUNDS OF NATURE (BY A WINDOW, PERHAPS) AND DRAW WHAT YOU HEAR, COMING UP WITH YOUR OWN VISUAL LANGUAGE FOR SOUNDS.

For example, a green dot for a duck's quack, a red wave for the wind, etc. Or you could move your pencil on the paper intuitively, trying to emulate the sound: loud, large, close, distant, moving away from you, high, deep or rumbling. Fill in the page until you feel you have captured an abstract soundscape.

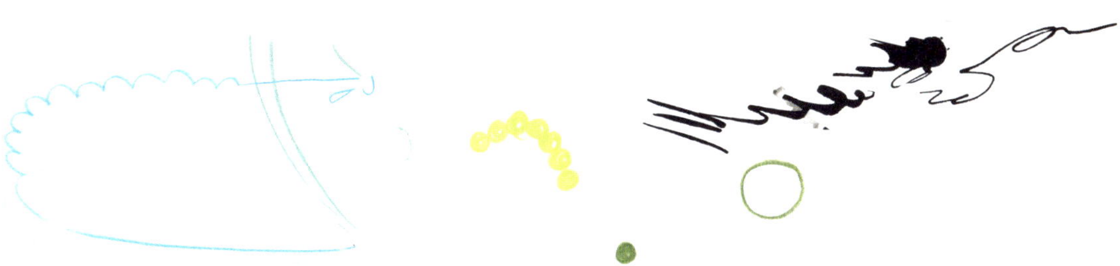

FILL THIS TILE WALL WITH DRAWINGS OF FLOWERS, BIRDS AND ANIMALS USING A BLUE PENCIL OR MARKER.

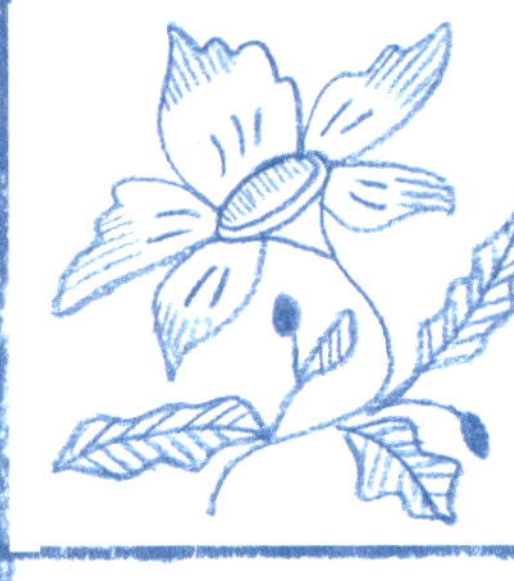

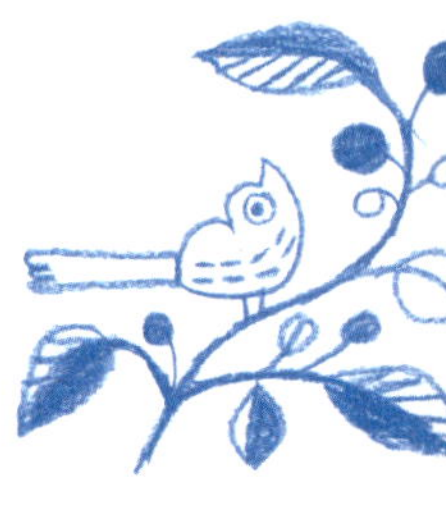

DRAW A COSY WINTER SCENE USING A LIMITED COLOUR PALETTE.

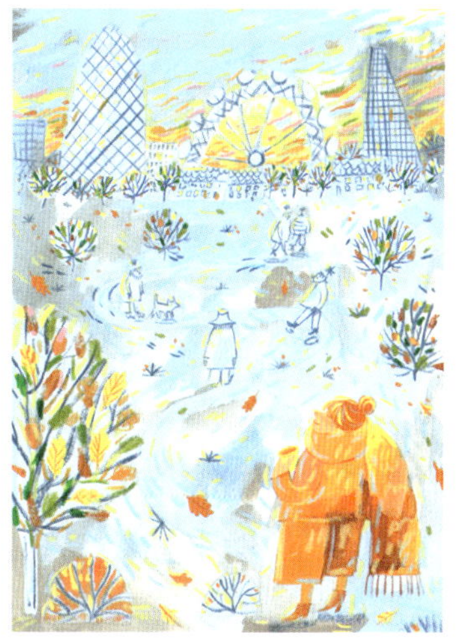

DRAW THE SAME MOTIF USING THE DIFFERENT COLOUR SCHEMES PROVIDED FOR YOU HERE TO SEE HOW COLOUR AFFECTS THE ARTWORK.

Try drawing a field with a tree or a view from your window.

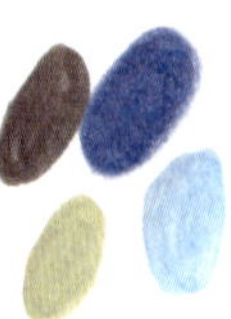

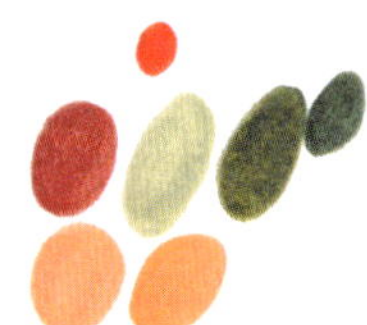

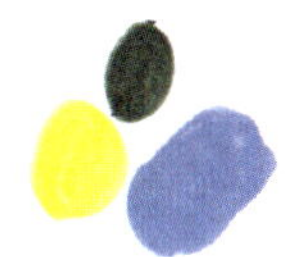

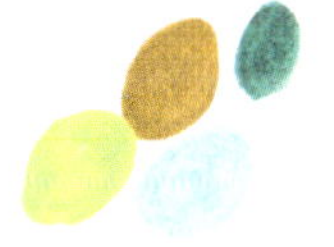

A GREAT WAY TO MIX UP A COMPOSITION IS TO ADD SOME GEOMETRIC SHAPES – THEY WILL ADD A FUN RHYTHM TO THE PICTURE.

Fill in this park scene with people, a fountain with swans swimming there, buildings in the background, trees, mountains and clouds. Work with one colour and think about line and texture.

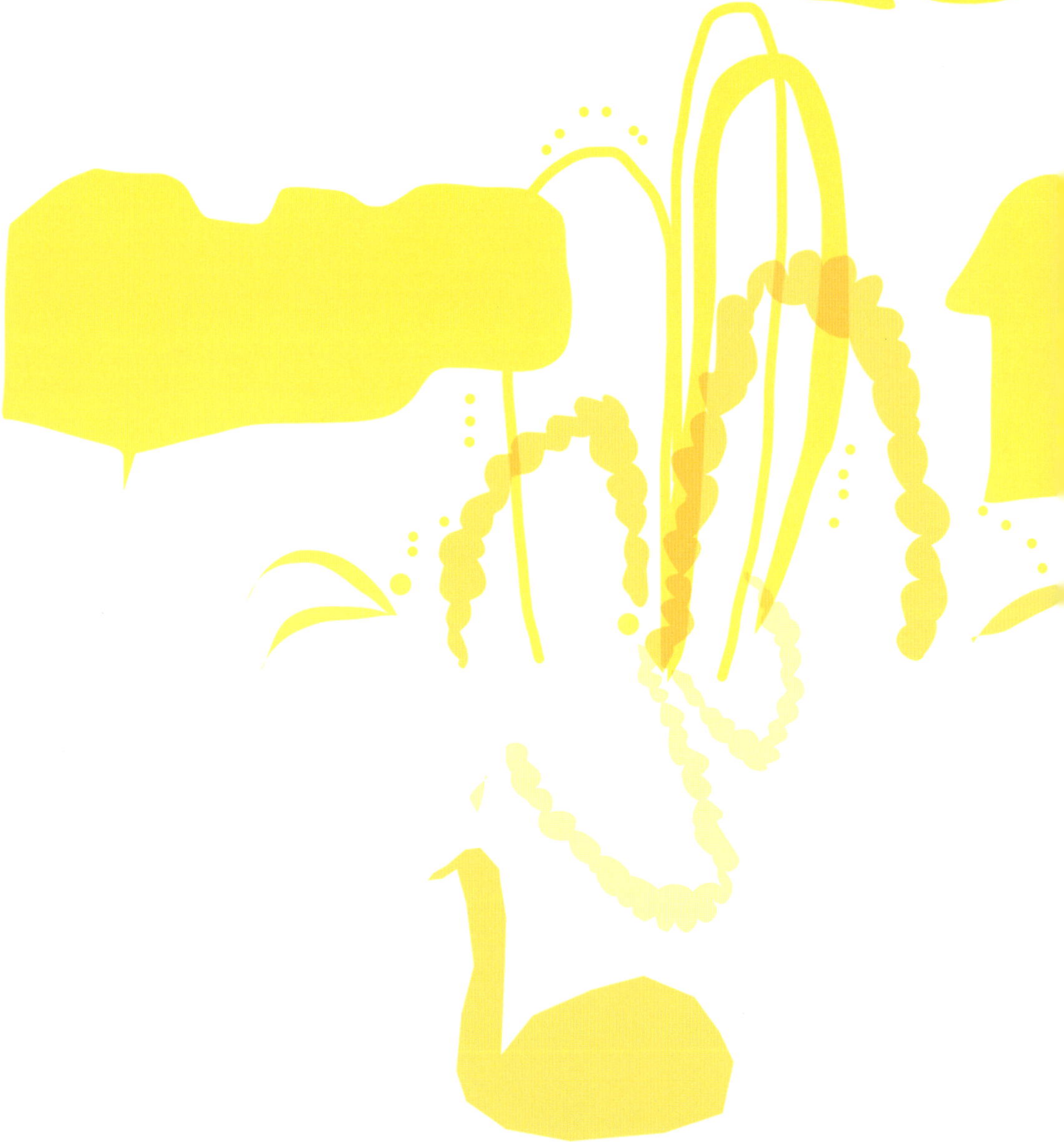

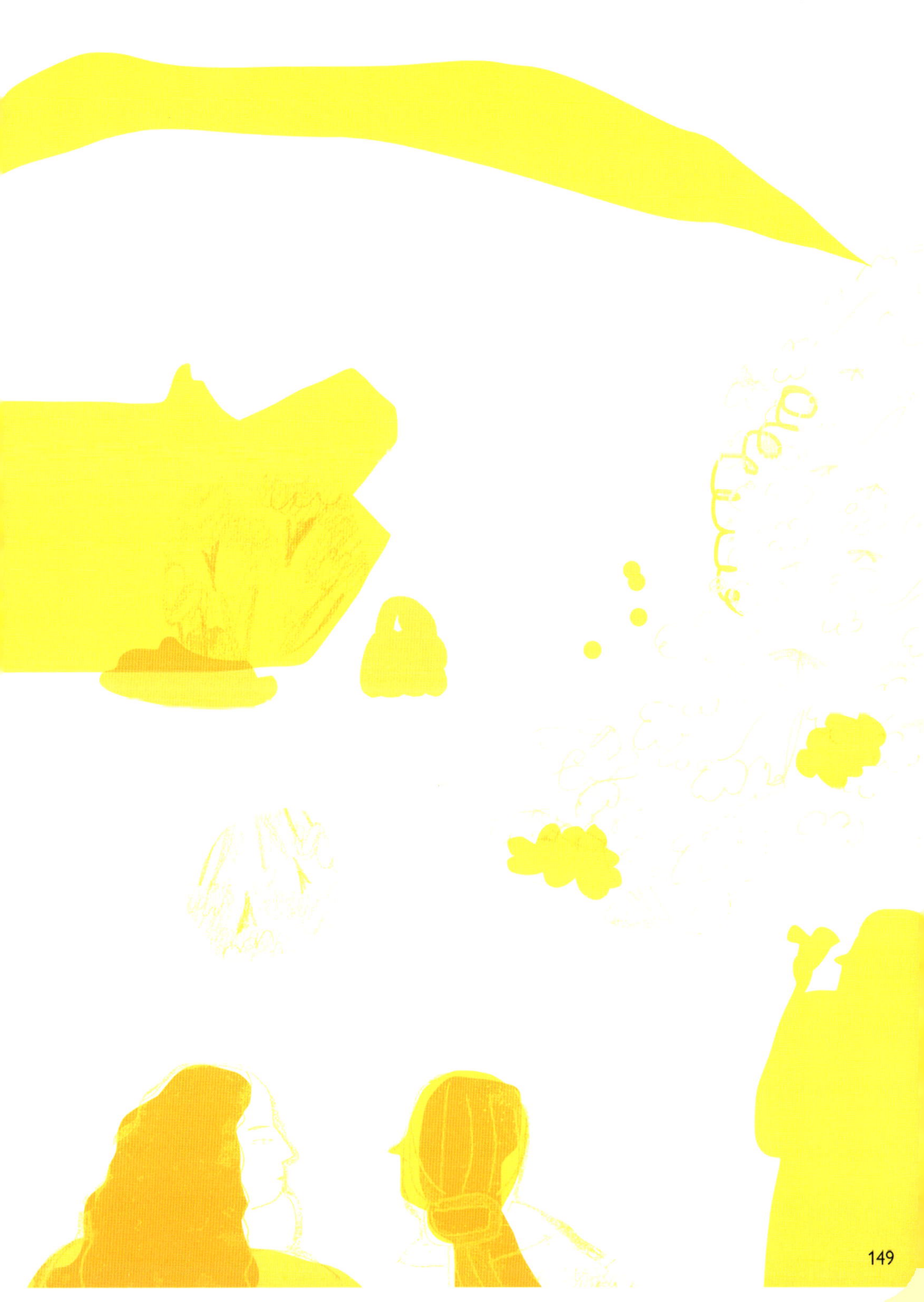

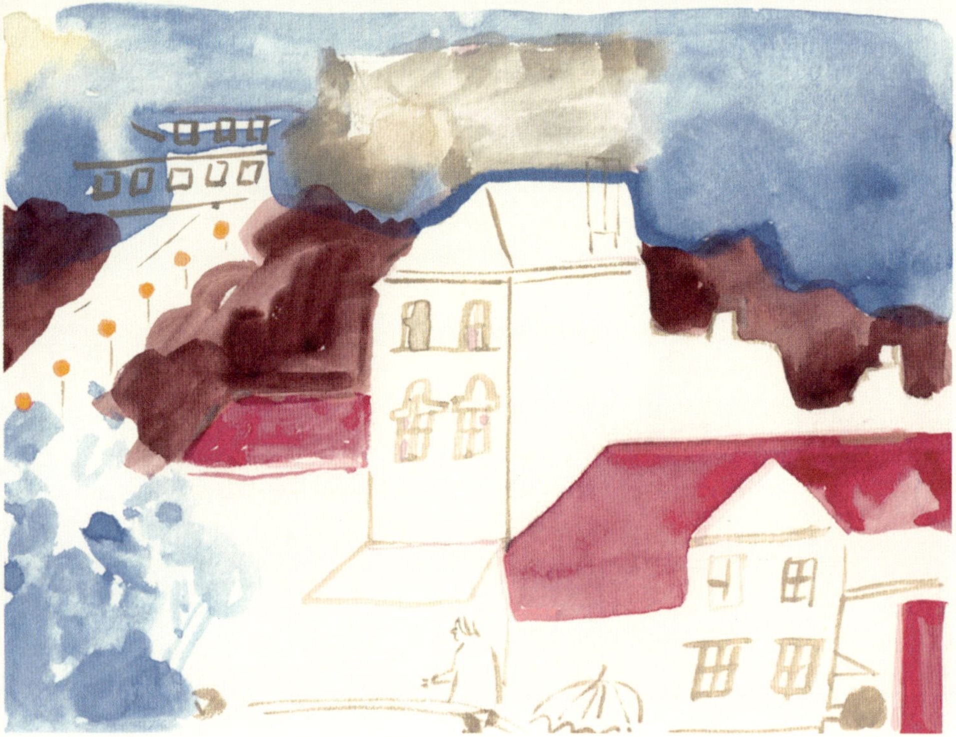

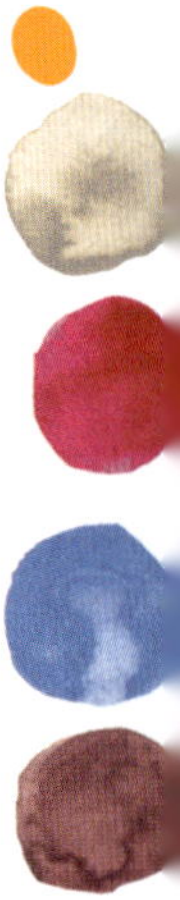

IT'S REALLY FUN TO EXPERIMENT WITH UNUSUAL COLOURS, EVEN WHEN YOU ARE DRAWING FROM LIFE.

This approach adds character and atmosphere to a drawing. Try changing the colours but matching the colour relationship based on tonality.

TO MAKE A PICTURE LOOK AS IF IT HAS ENERGY AND MOVEMENT, WE HAVE TO FEEL THAT ENERGY AND GENERATE THE MOVEMENT WITH OUR HAND WHEN DRAWING.

Let's try now. Choose a reference – a picture of a forest or some trees – set a timer for 10 minutes and create a drawing based on that reference.

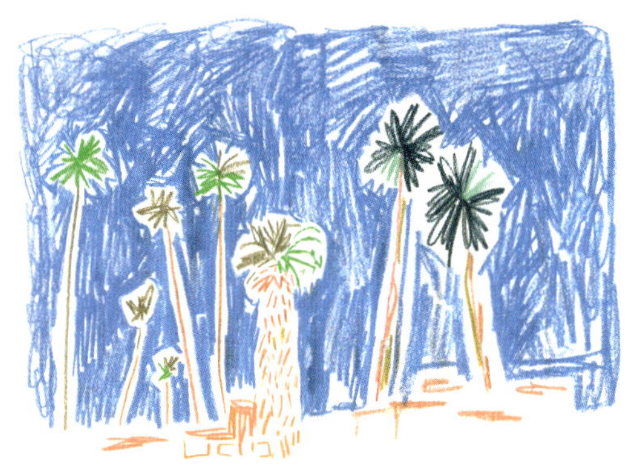

90

MOUNTAIN VIEW STEP-BY-STEP

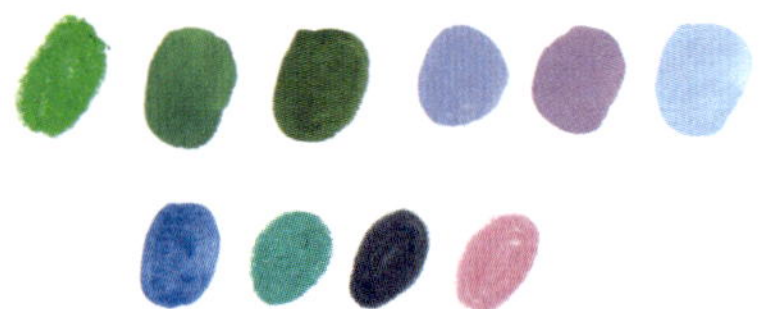

MATERIALS:
A4 sheet of paper
Graphite pencil
Paints, markers or colouring pencils in colours similar to swatches

STEP 1

Sketch out a composition on paper. Draw several mountain peaks, rolling hills and some islands in the distance. And a person and dog standing in the foreground.

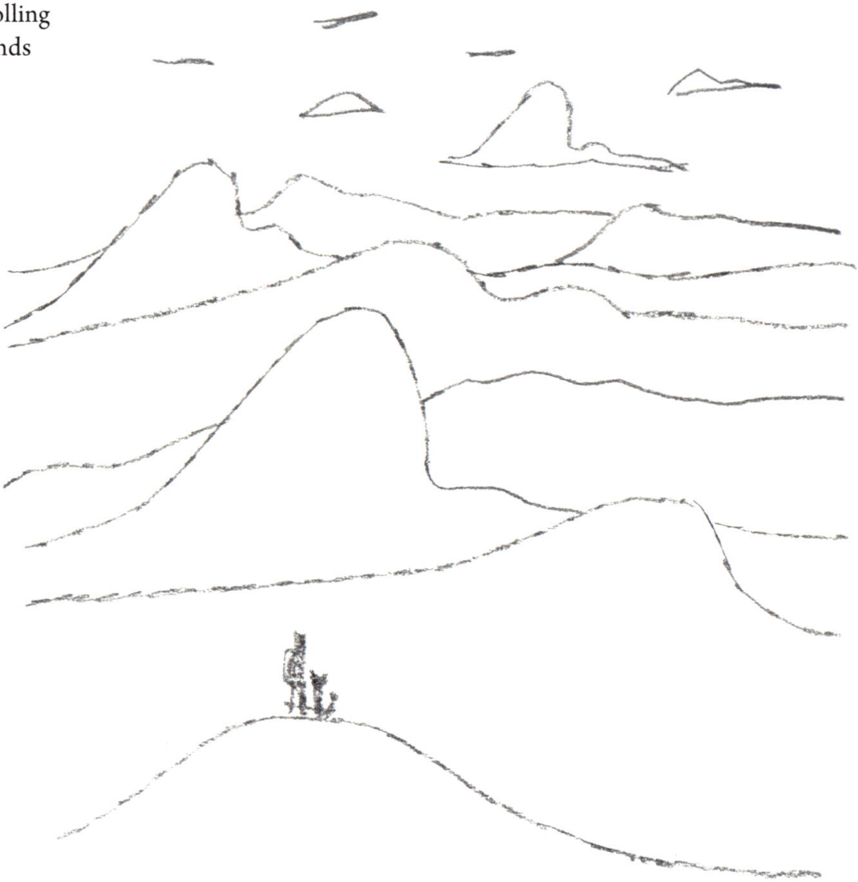

STEP 2

Take a deep green and fill in the first hill in the foreground.

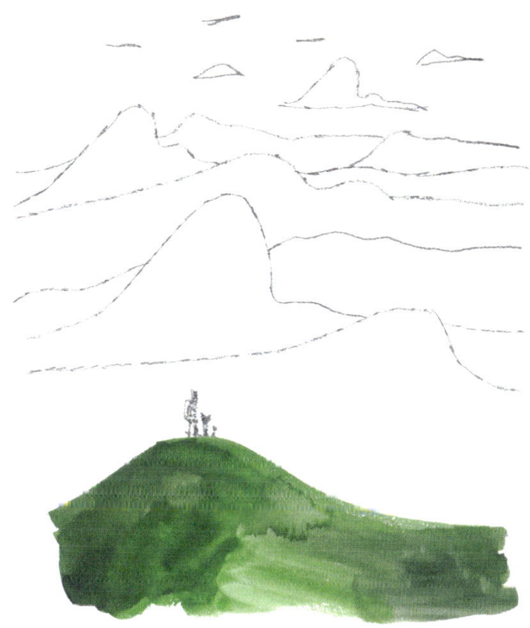

STEP 3

Now fill in the second mountain using a lighter green. Don't paint over the first hill, but allow some space between the two.

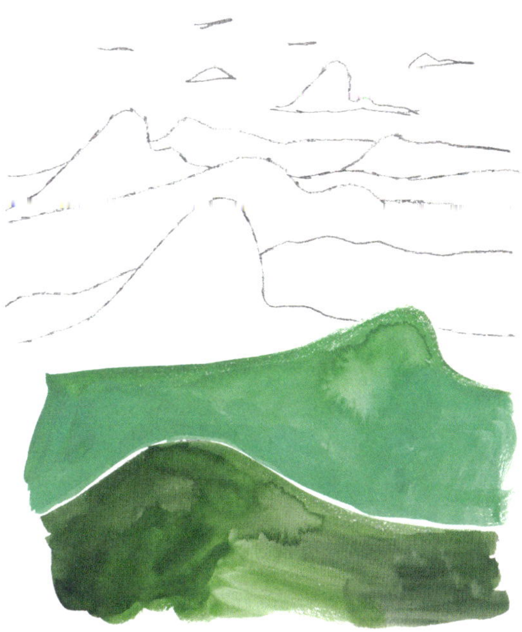

STEP 4

Using blue, paint another peak, this time changing up the shape. Maybe this one will have the highest peak? Continue filling in more mountains in different colours.

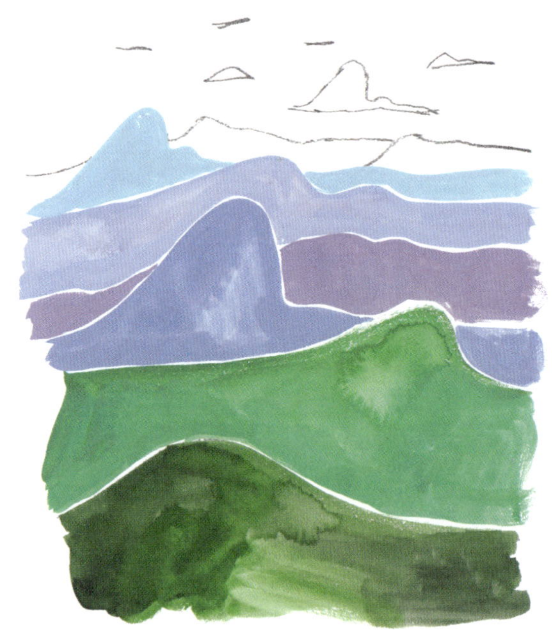

STEP 5

Using colouring pencils, paints or markers, draw the outline of more of the mountains as they move further into the distance. Colour in the islands in the background, too.

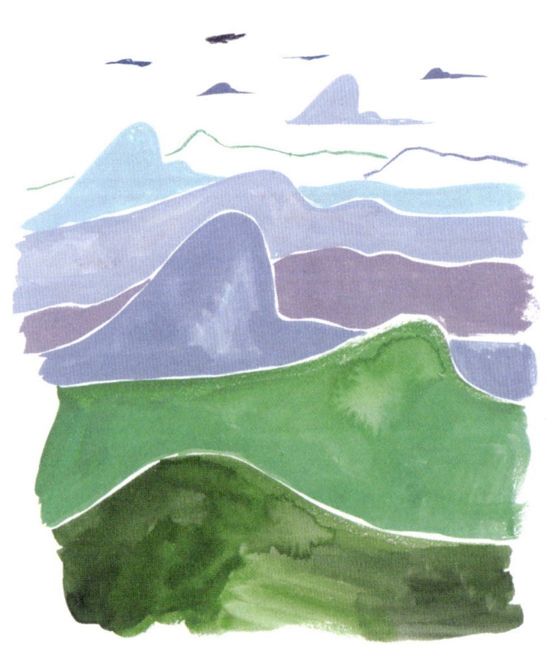

STEP 6

Using a dark green, similar to the one you used to paint the mountain in step one, paint the person and dog standing on top of the first hill overlooking the view.

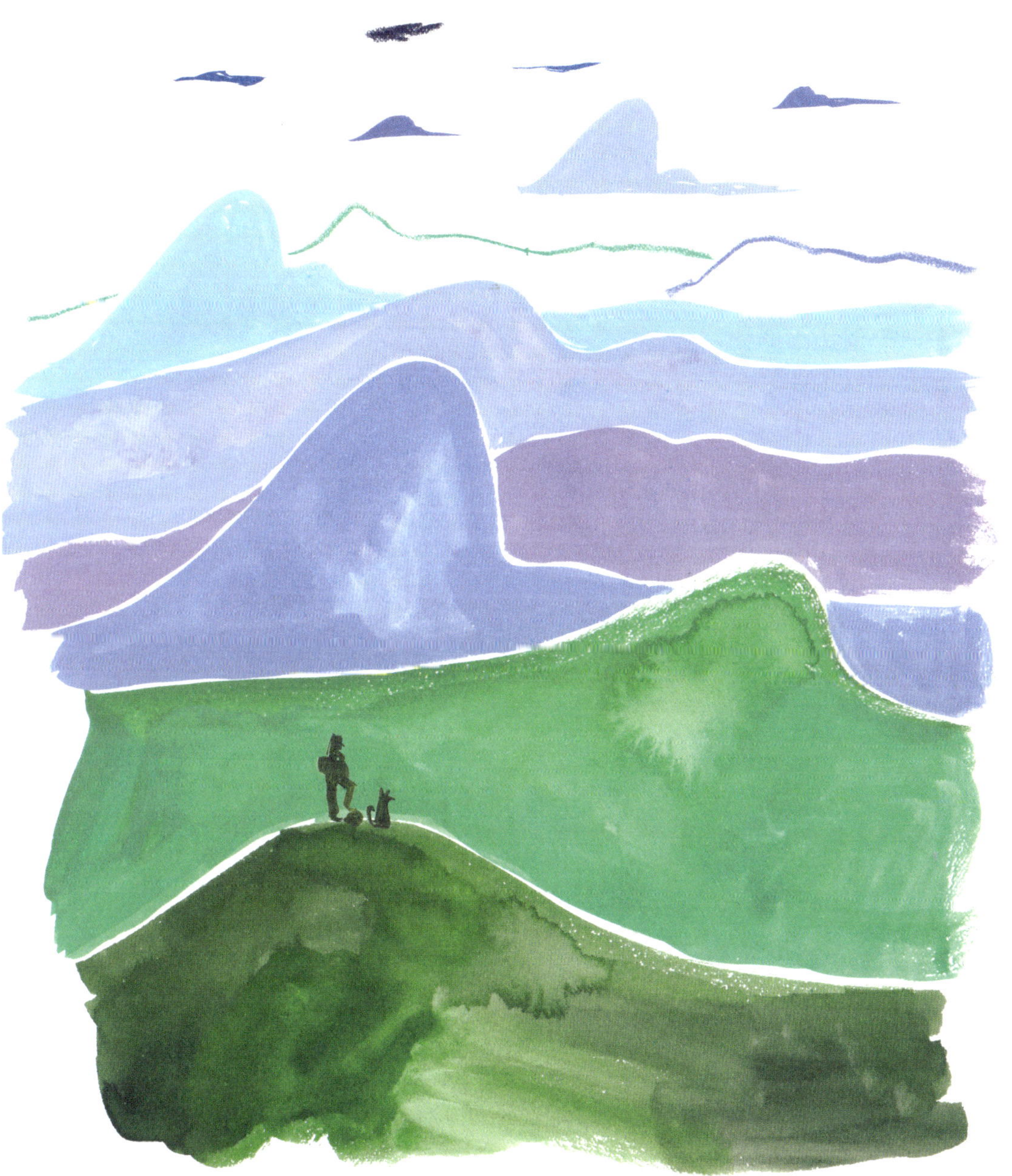

USE A REFERENCE PHOTO OF YOUR CHOICE AS A STARTING POINT TO CREATE A SERIES OF SKETCHES, BUT CHANGE UP THE COMPOSITION, CROP, SUBJECT, PERSPECTIVE, LAYOUT AND PROPORTIONS TO HELP YOU HIGHLIGHT DIFFERENT ASPECTS OF THE IMAGE AND ALLOW YOU TO MAKE ALL THE CREATIVE DECISIONS.

I have sketched a photo of a beautiful Moroccan palace with palm trees, but I changed the perspective from linear to orthographic, framed the roof and sky, the corner of the palace and fountain, birds and palm trees, and changed the proportion of the image to an extra-long portrait format.

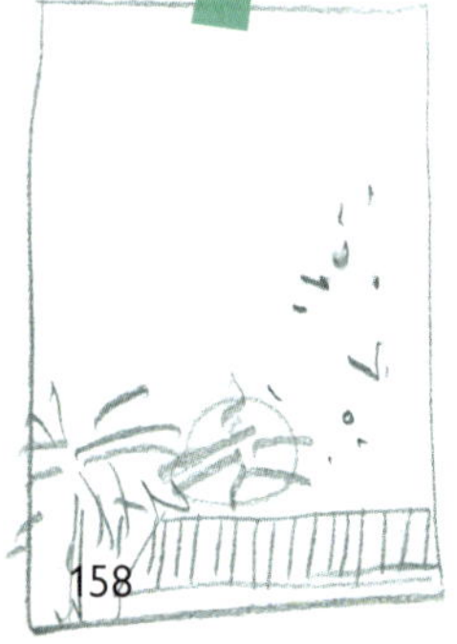

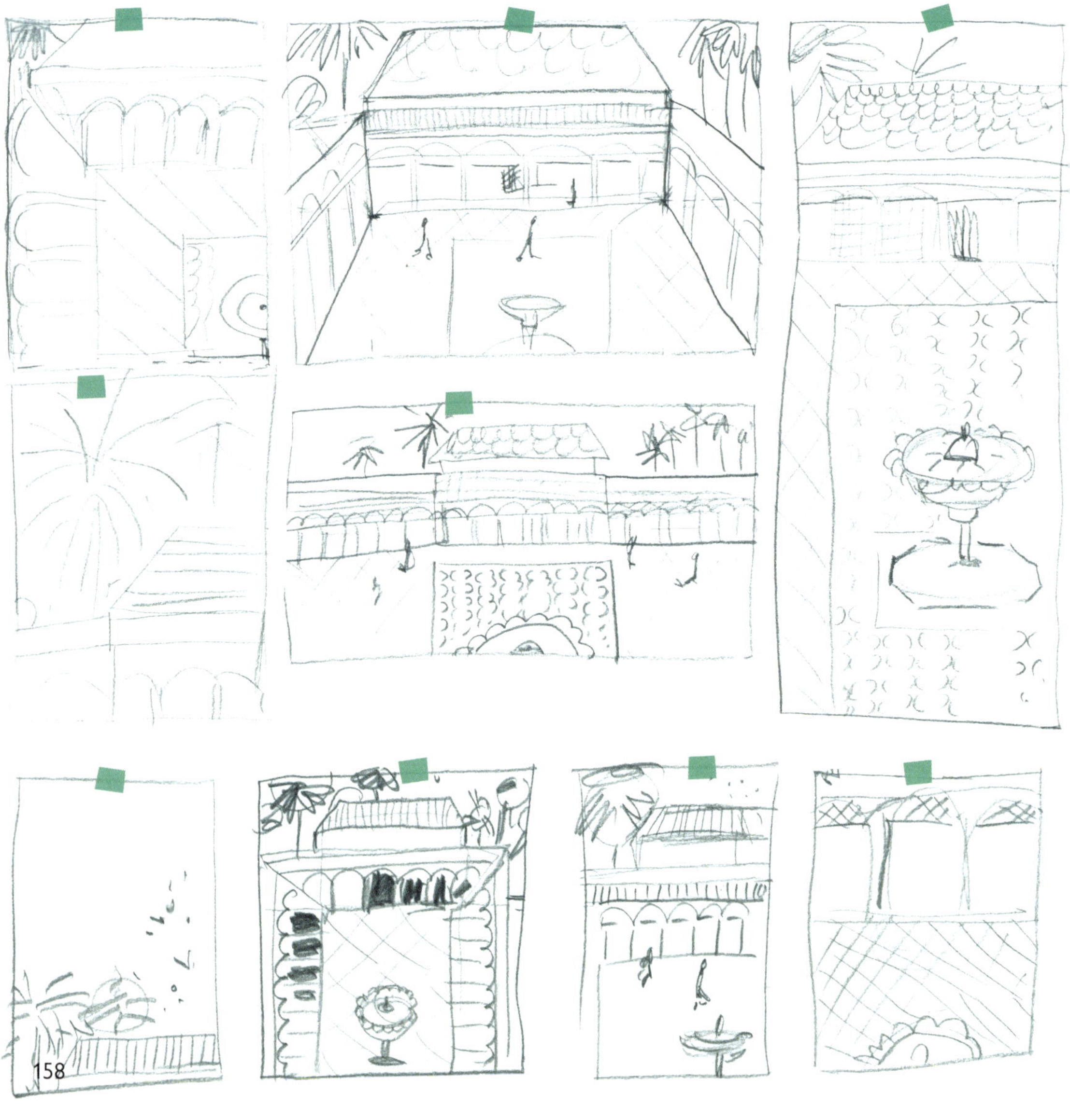

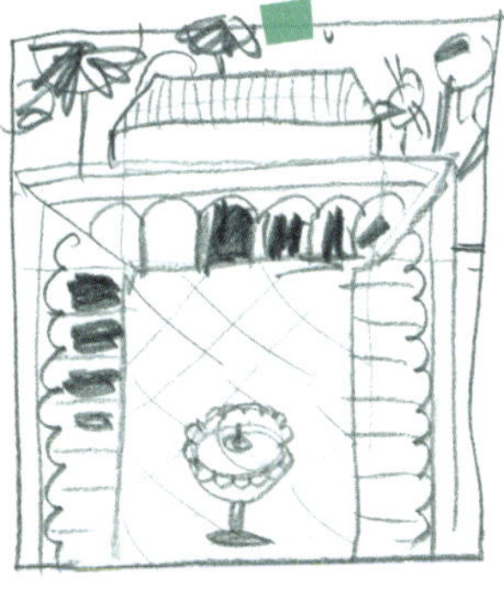

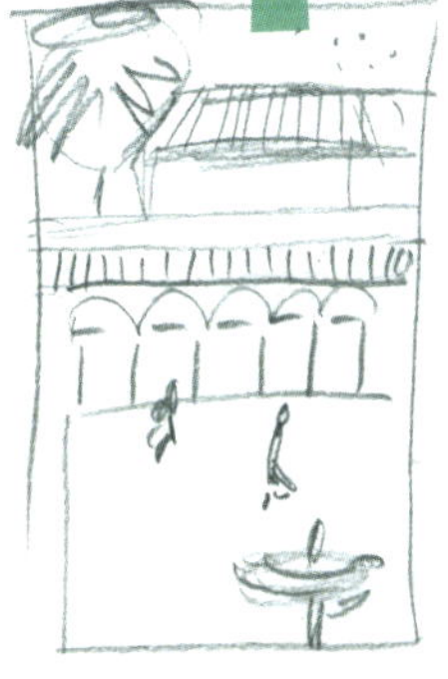

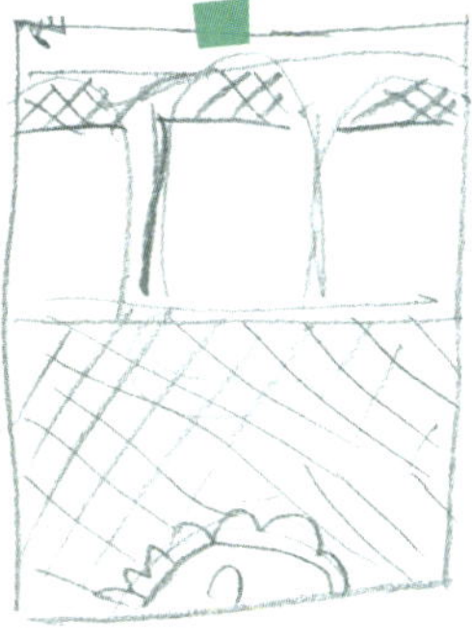

DRAW THE LANDSCAPE FOR THE ARTIST ON THE CANVAS AS WELL AS THE LANDSCAPE FROM WHICH THEY'RE TAKING INSPIRATION.

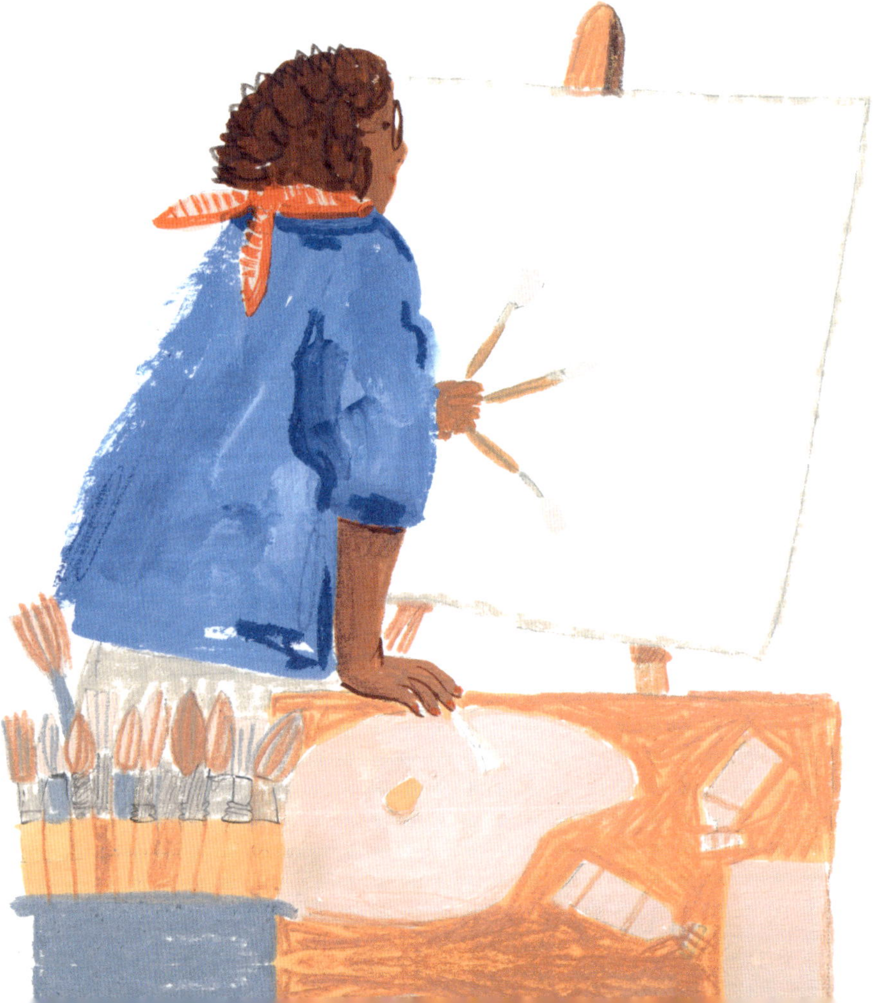

COMPOSITION IS ONE OF MY FAVOURITE ASPECTS OF DRAWING, AS IT CAN COMMUNICATE MOOD, ENERGY, FEELING AND SIZE AND PROVIDES AN ENDLESS OPPORTUNITY FOR EXPERIMENTATION.

By creating these thumbnails, you will have a nice library of different compositions, which you can use in the future to help you create real objects. The spiky shape could form a tree-line or clouds, or maybe fruits and leaves. Come up with your own abstract shapes and work in one colour.

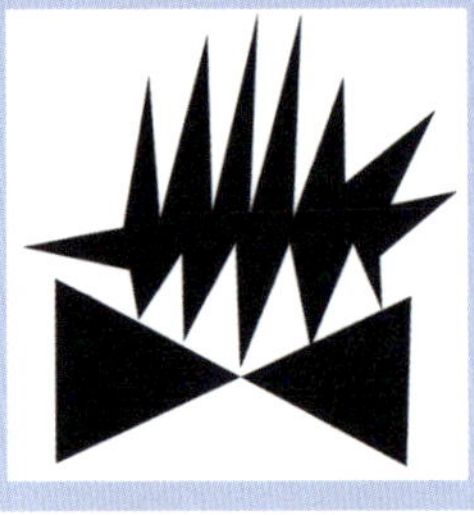

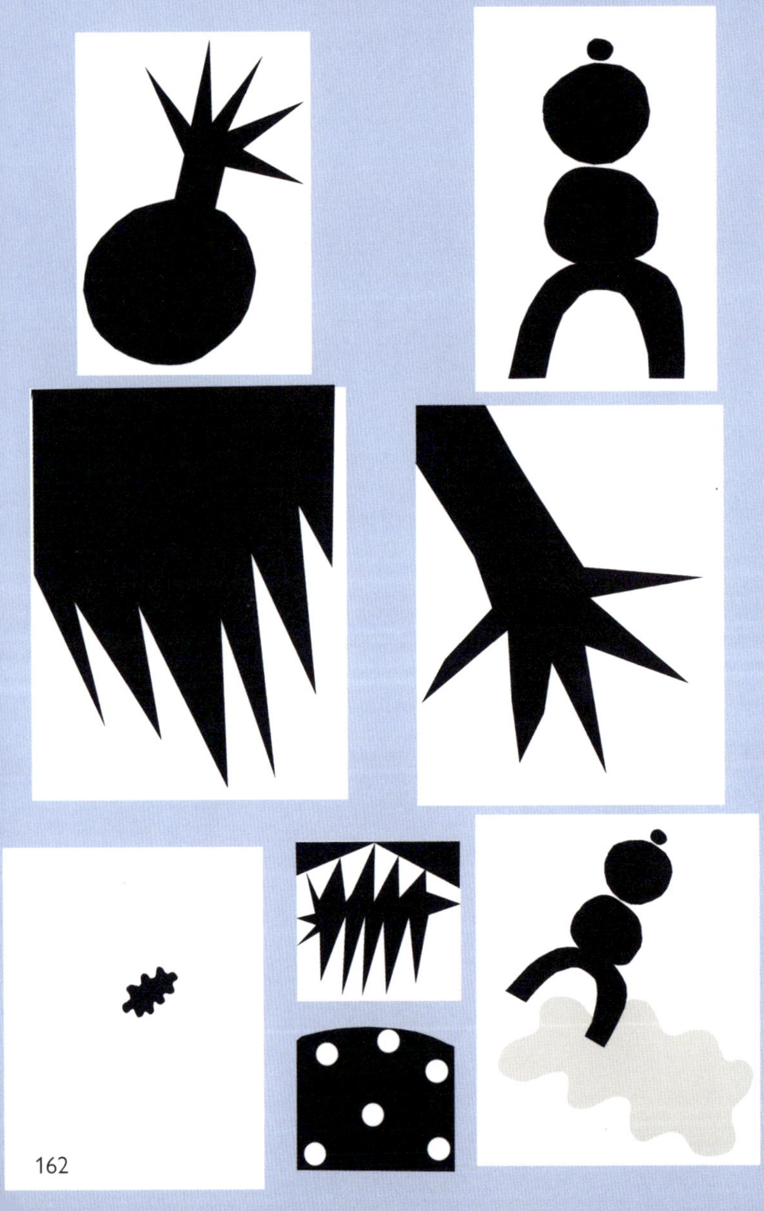

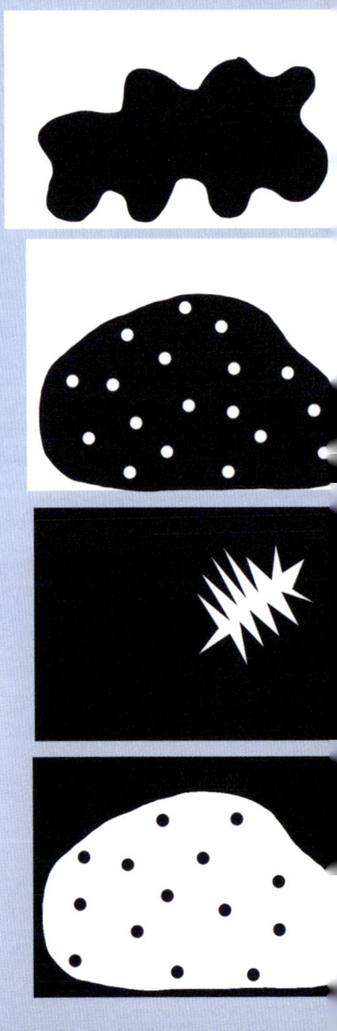

THERE ARE MANY WAYS TO COMMUNICATE WHAT IS THE MOST IMPORTANT PART OF A DRAWING AND TO MAKE IT STAND OUT.

One approach is to draw the prominent object using colour while keeping the background neutral. In this example, the tulip bouquet is the focal point. I have used bright colours for the blooms and stems, then used pencil only to draw the surrounding scene. Why don't you have a go?

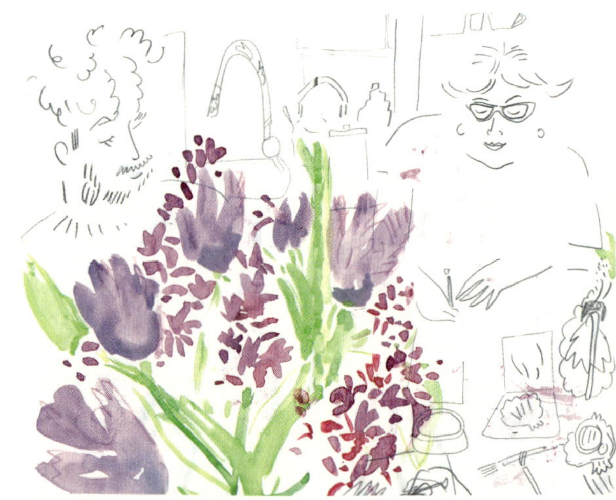

LET'S TAKE AN OPPOSITE APPROACH IN THIS EXAMPLE. To make the lighthouse stand out, I have kept the colours quite muted with a simple outline and minimal detail. Then the rest of the picture is bright and bold with colour, patterns and plenty of mark making.

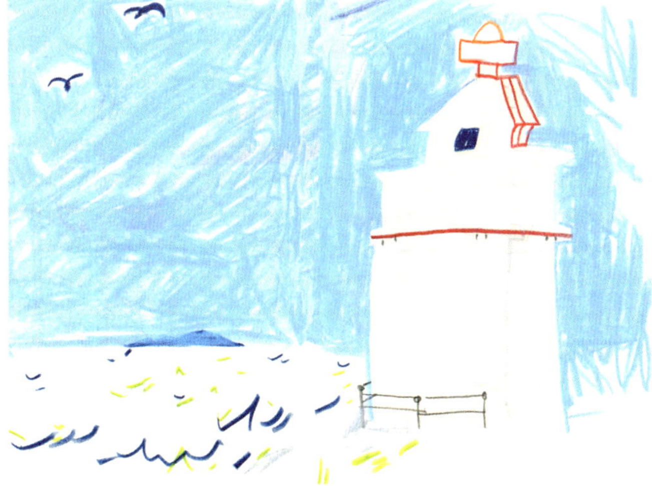

USING AN IMAGE AS REFERENCE, DRAW A SERIES OF THUMBNAILS TO PLAY WITH COMPOSITION.

The image can be a photo from a holiday or an editorial spread from a magazine.

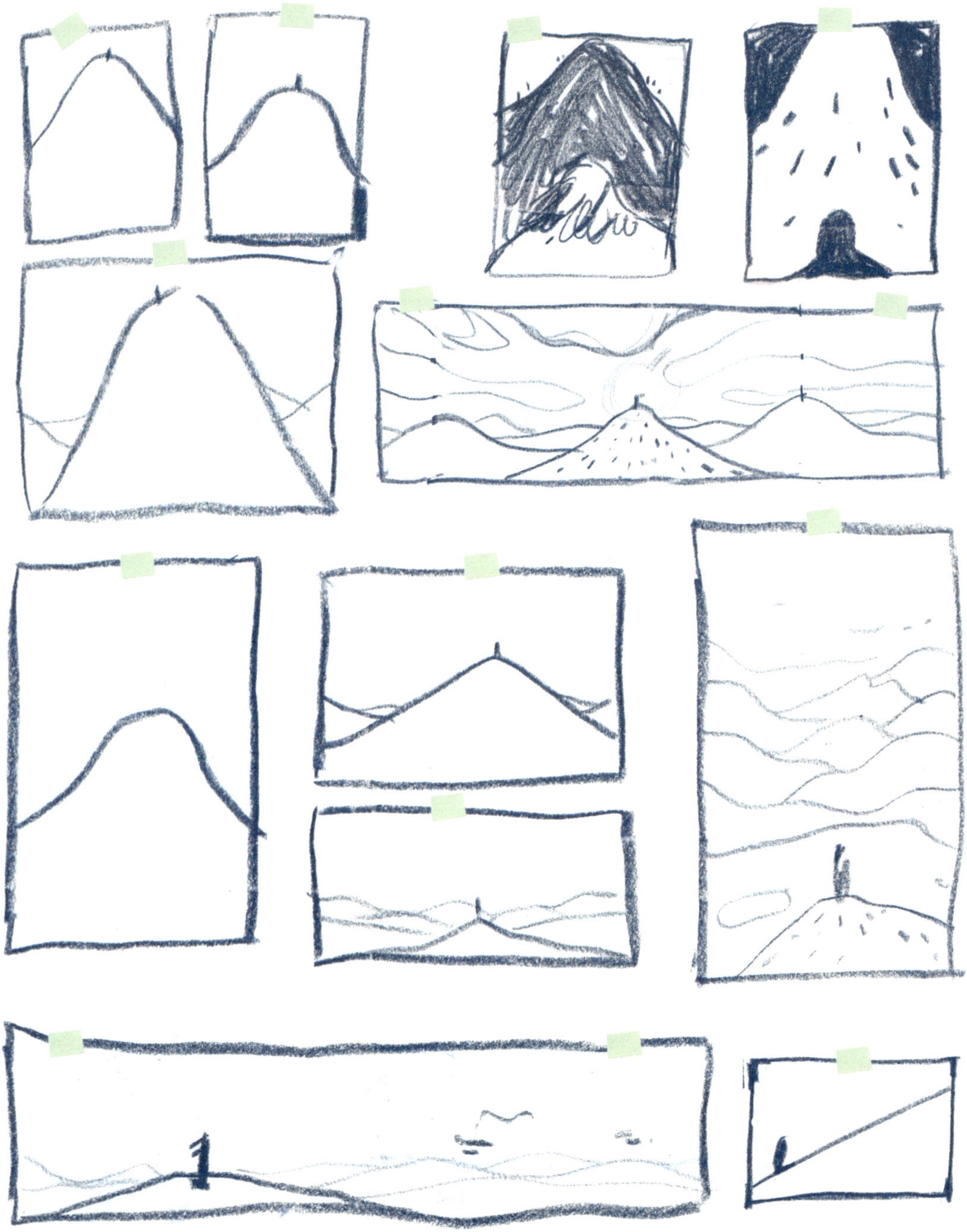

Draw what happens when you crop out certain parts of the image. Include what you can't see. Draw what you think happened before this moment and what is going to happen in the next few moments. Change up the format of your thumbnails, too – long, square or thin, close up or from far away – and see how many different variations you can create.

SIT YOURSELF CLOSE TO NATURE AND START TO DRAW YOUR SURROUNDINGS.

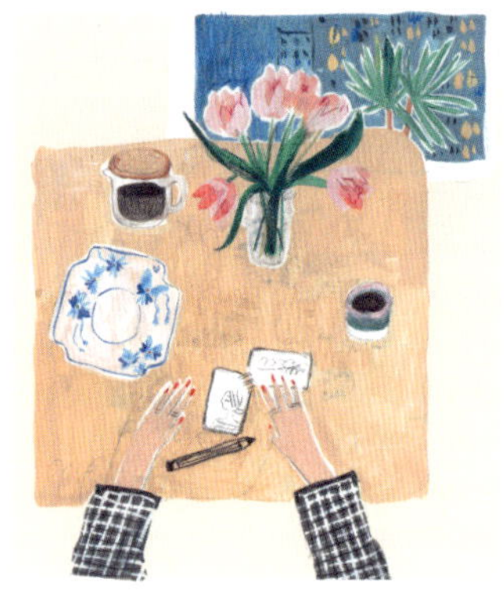

CREATE A QUICK LANDSCAPE COLLAGE USING ANY COLOURED PAPER YOU HAVE.

Feel free to add paper from old train tickets, receipts and magazines! Maybe you will make a mountain, a bouquet of flowers or a field. Work quickly and be bold. Think about shapes and colours!

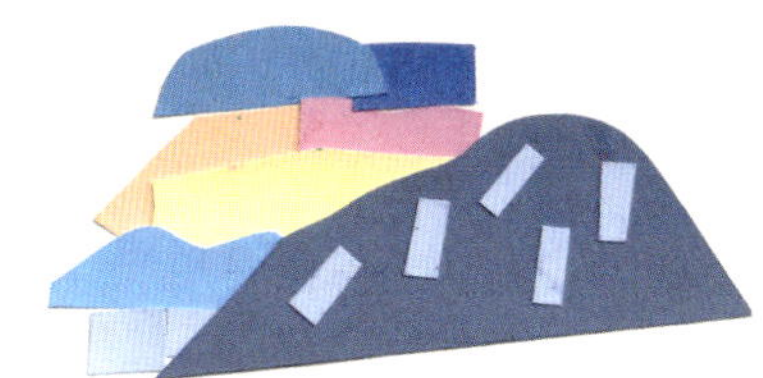

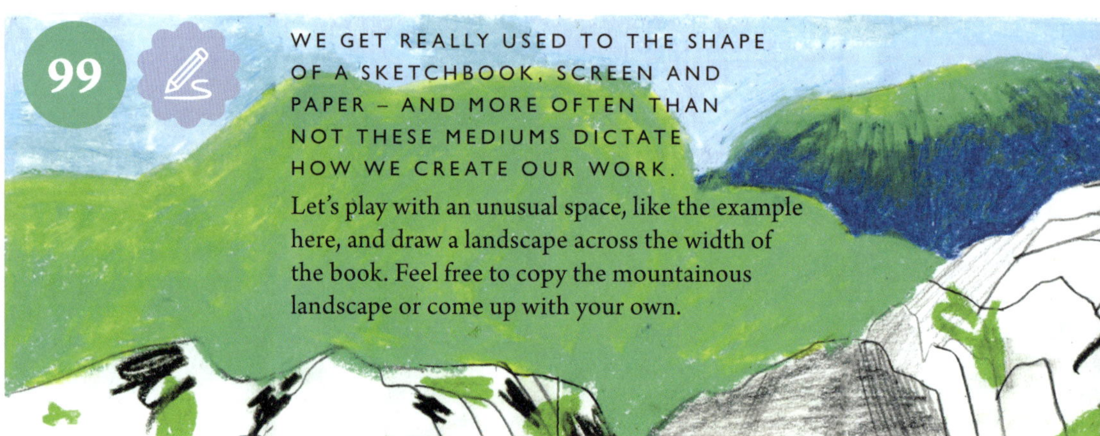

99

WE GET REALLY USED TO THE SHAPE OF A SKETCHBOOK, SCREEN AND PAPER – AND MORE OFTEN THAN NOT THESE MEDIUMS DICTATE HOW WE CREATE OUR WORK.

Let's play with an unusual space, like the example here, and draw a landscape across the width of the book. Feel free to copy the mountainous landscape or come up with your own.

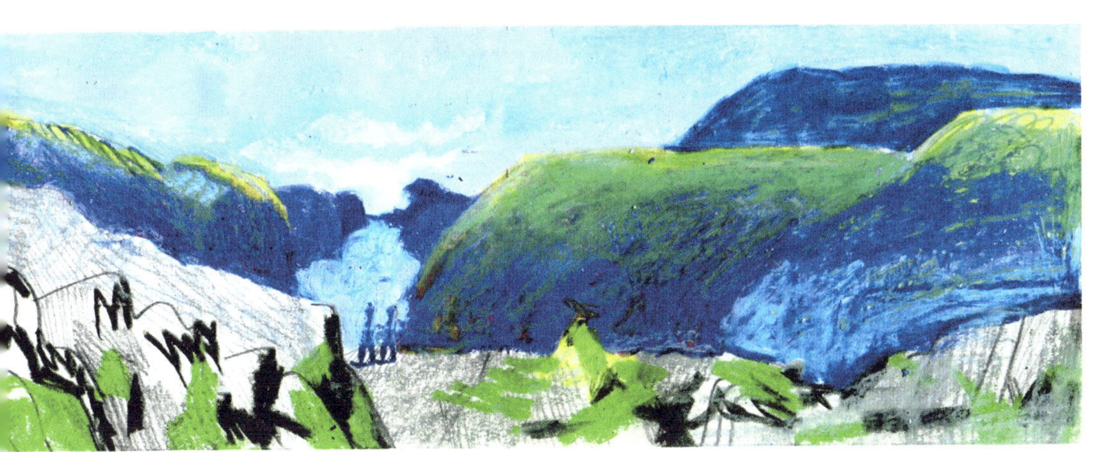

LET'S FINISH THIS BOOK WITH A SUNSET, A PLAYFUL DISPLAY OF MARKS AND A BEAUTIFUL SHOW OF COLOUR.

Draw your favourite sunset, be free, mark make, add more colour and have fun!

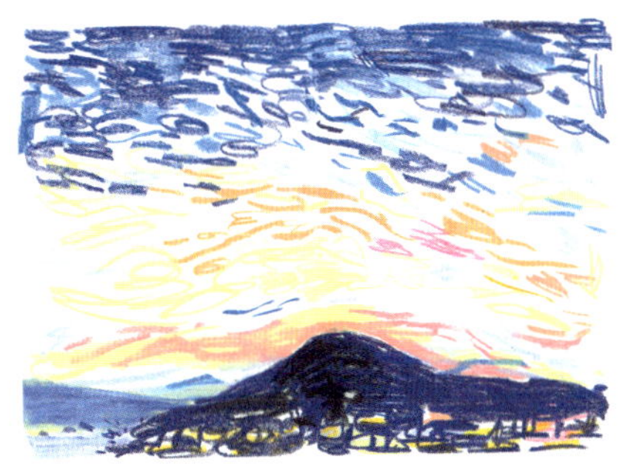

About the Author

VIKTORIJA SEMJONOVA

Viktorija is a Latvian illustrator and designer, now based in Bergen, Norway.

Having studied and lived in London, UK, Viktorija draws inspiration from diverse artistic influences.

With a passion for drawing from observation, she specialises in creating illustrations for publications and products using traditional materials such as gouache, pencils and pastels.

She has taught workshops at the Victoria and Albert Museum and shared her knowledge of drawing people both in person and online. She is passionate about encouraging everyone to get drawing and be creative without limits.

Viktorija has created illustrations and worked on a range of creative projects with Pinterest, Ovarian Cancer Action, Global Citizen, YouTube, Swatch, Tombow, kikki K and various book publishers.

Acknowledgements

THANK YOU TO...

My editor Kate, for believing in this book, for all of the advice and creativity. To Claire, for the design and for making this book look so beautiful. And to everyone at Quadrille, for all their hard work and making this book a reality!

Thank you to my sister Nikita, for being a source of creative inspiration, to my parents Anželika and Sergejs, for teaching us to stay curious. *Tusen takk* to my partner Ole for the coffee and constant support. And to all my illustration colleagues for the pep talks and a supportive community.

And to YOU, my dear readers, for drawing along, for your support – thank you so very much!

Quadrille, Penguin Random House UK,
One Embassy Gardens, 8 Viaduct Gardens,
London SW11 7BW

Quadrille Publishing Limited is part of the Penguin Random House group of companies whose addresses can be found at global.penguinrandomhouse.com

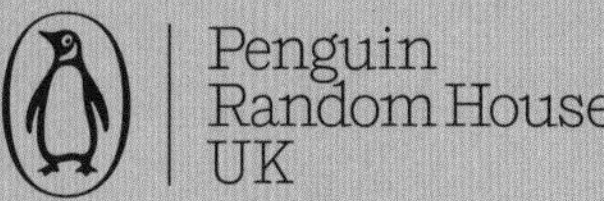

Published by Quadrille in 2025

www.penguin.co.uk

A CIP catalogue record for this book is available from the British Library

ISBN: 9781784887872
10 9 8 7 6 5 4 3 2 1

Publishing Director: Kajal Mistry
Senior Commissioning Editor: Kate Burkett
Design: Claire Warner Studio
Photography: Maryna Kolpakova
Copy-editor and Proofreader: Caroline West
Production Controller: Martina Georgieva

Colour Reproduction by p2d

Printed in China by
C&C Offset Printing Co., Ltd

The authorised representative in the EEA is Penguin Random House Ireland, Morrison Chambers, 32 Nassau Street, Dublin D02 YH68.

Penguin Random House is committed to a sustainable future for our business, our readers and our planet. This book is made from Forest Stewardship Council® certified paper.